SETCLAE
Self-Esteem Through Culture Leads to Academic Excellence
High School Workbook

First Edition
Fourth Printing
Author
    Folami Prescott
Major Consultant
    Jawanza Kunjufu

Chicago, Illinois

Acknowledgements

All praises due to the creator.

Special thanks to my family, extended and otherwise,
for their support manifested by babysitting, cooking, praising,
criticizing, encouraging, and brainstorming!

Thanks to Jawanza
for having vision and insight
that we could produce
such a comprehensive and necessary curriculum as SETCLAE.
And for having such <u>high expectations</u>
of my ability to complete this tremendous task.

Thanks <u>most of all</u> to my children,
Yakini and Issa,
for being big sister and brother to High School SETCLAE
and to Nana Kwesi
for being my partner through it all
in ALL WAYS.

Give thanks and praise.

Asante sana.

Sister Folami

THE SETCLAE WORKBOOK
HIGH SCHOOL/POST-SECONDARY

TABLE OF CONTENTS

Introduction

Habari Gani? If you use this workbook to its fullest extent, you will soon know what this Kiswahili phrase means, and use the phrase to greet your friends and family.

Habari gani means "What's the news?" in Kiswahili. If you are feeling fine, you may respond "Mzuri" (good) or "Njema" (fine).

Asante Sana. Habari gani? (Thank you very much and how are you?)

And I would respond "Njema. Asante sana. Hofu Ni kwenu." (Fine. Thank you very much. My concern is for you.)

That our concern is for you will become very clear as you continue to use this workbook. It offers a great deal of information, activities, exercises, and ideas for you to use to learn from and share with others. In fact, many of the activities must be carried out with others. Working in Harambee circles, you and your peers, family members, and other concerned extended family members will learn, sing, dance, act, write, discuss, think, and grow as you explore some of the most critical issues concerning and affecting African people. (HARAMBEE means "let's pull together" in Kiswahili.)

You will address the meaning of your favorite songs, relationships with your friends and family, your feelings about school, what it means to be a man or a woman, and some very important and enlightening lessons regarding African and African American history and culture.

There are TEN CRITICAL QUESTIONS which follow this introduction that everyone should be able to answer. We would like you to answer them now and again after using this book. We guarantee you will be pleased with your own levels of growth and heightened awareness of self, your environment, and the world around you.

In addition to the major activity for each issue addressed, there is additional information and activities to be used by you and your peers, family, and teachers. And don't forget that we are all teachers! As long as we communicate with other people in some form or fashion, we are teaching! And if we are soaking in the communication of others, we are learning!

Everyone is a "Mwalimu Mwanafunzi" (teacher-student).

To get the full benefits from this guide to exploring and improving your self and your community, you will need the following materials:

The following books by Dr. Jawanza Kunjufu

Lessons From History, Jr./Sr. High
Motivating and Preparing Black Youth to Work
To Be Popular or Smart
The following videos by Dr. Jawanza Kunjufu:

To Be Popular or Smart
Lessons From History/Roots: A Street Life Analysis

The materials you will need for each Harambee Time are referred to at the introduction of each topic.

There are other publications and audio-visuals that would be helpful but are not absolutely necessary. However, we hope you will utilize your resources (libraries, school, friends, etc.) as well as continue to build your own library of African and African American History Culture.

There is one thing you must do before you go any further:

Let your KUUMBA (creativity) flow!!!

1. Get familiar with the Kiswahili words used in an effort to spread the language that was chosen as the Pan-African language by the Pan-African conference in 1974. (Pan-African refers to all people of African descent all around the world.)

2. When coloring materials are needed, use a variety to include markers, paints, crayons, tissue paper, and whatever you can get your hands on.

3. Use magazines such as Ebony, Essence, Jet, Emerge, African Commentary, Black Enterprise, and other publications. They are filled with information and illustrations of Black Life.

4. Use your ideas to create poems, raps, skits, songs, dances, dramatic presentations, speeches, plays, essays, books, and letters to share all of your insight with others.

5. Use the workbook as a journal. Use the space after the quotation or proverb introducing each topic to write your interpretation of that thought.

6. Write down many of your concerns, ideas, questions, and brainstorms.

7. Always remember: everyone is a mwalimu manafunzi (teacher student).

8. Never forget what SETCLAE stands for: Self-Esteem Through Culture Leads to Academic Excellence!!!

HARAMBEE!!!
(Let's pull together!)

PAMOJA TUTASHINDA!!!
(Together we will win!)

TEN CRITICAL QUESTIONS
(WHAT EVERY STUDENT WILL KNOW AFTER SETCLAE)

1. Who am I?

2. Where did my people originate?

3. When did the history of my people begin?

4. What have my people contributed?

5. What is the culture of my people?

6. Who oppressed my people?

7. How was it done? (oppression of an African people)

8. How did my people respond?

9. What is the present condition of my people?

10. What can I do to enhance the condition of my people?

The SETCLAE Student Profile

High School/Post-Secondary

Instructions

Please answer the following questions on the answer sheet and think real hard about how you really feel before answering each one. THERE ARE NO RIGHT OR WRONG ANSWERS. We want YOUR answers.

Part I

Read each statement or question. If it is true for you, select the answer "a" on the answer sheet. If it is not true for you, select the answer "b". Answer every question even if it's hard to decide. (Just think about yourself and what's important to you.) Select only one answer for each question.

1. I like to be alone sometimes.	a. Yes	b. No
2. I enjoy public speaking.	a. Yes	b. No
3. Cleaning up should be done collectively.	a. Yes	b. No
4. School will help me to accomplish my own goals.	a. Yes	b. No
5. I enjoy looking for positive things to say about people.	a. Yes	b. No
6. I have personal goals.	a. Yes	b. No
7. I would rather do an extra credit project by myself than with a small group.	a. Yes	b. No
8. I get upset when things don't go my way.	a. Yes	b. No
9. School is boring most of the time.	a. Yes	b. No
10. I speak more than one dialect.	a. Yes	b. No
11. If I don't see a trash can, I throw my trash on the ground.	a. Yes	b. No
12. I like participating in special projects like science fairs and quiz bowls.	a. Yes	b. No
13. When the truth is hard to say, I don't say it.	a. Yes	b. No
14. My friends are more important to me than my family.	a. Yes	b. No
15. My neighborhood is a good place to live.	a. Yes	b. No
16. I can get any job I want if I work at it hard enough.	a. Yes	b. No
17. I like being with people that are different from me.	a. Yes	b. No
18. I like me!	a. Yes	b. No
19. I believe I can have my own business when I get older.	a. Yes	b. No

20. The contribution I make to the world is not as important as the contributions of some other more famous people.   a. Yes   b. No

21. African Americans have not made many achievements in math, science, technology, and business.   a. Yes   b. No

22. If I could, I would make friends with people of all races.   a. Yes   b. No

23. Black people are not able to compete with others in many areas.   a. Yes   b. No

24. I want to be able to speak standard English in certain situations.   a. Yes   b. No

Part II

Read each item carefully. If it is something that is important to you, select the "a" on the answer sheet. If it is not important to you (it doesn't really matter or has nothing to do with you), select the "b" box. Take your time and think about it. There are no right or wrong answers. We want to know your feelings.

1. Helping others

    a. Important to me   b. Not important to me

2. What others think of me

    a. Important to me   b. Not important to me

3. Reading in a study group

    a. Important to me   b. Not important to me

4. Television as a way to receive most of my information

    a. Important to me   b. Not important to me

5. Solving problems by fighting

    a. Important to me   b. Not important to me

6. Learning about my family Members - dead and living

    a. Important to me   b. Not important to me

7. Working with others on short- and long-term projects

    a. Important to me   b. Not important to me

8. Doing whatever my friends do

    a. Important to me   b. Not important to me

9. Wearing expensive clothes

    a. Important to me   b. Not important to me

10. Doing well in school

    a. Important to me   b. Not important to me

11. Speaking up for myself and my ideas

        a. Important to me   b. Not important to me

12. Being positive most of the time

        a. Important to me   b. Not important to me

13. Living conditions in Africa

        a. Important to me   b. Not important to me

Part III

Read each statement carefully. Read the choices. Then select "a" if the statement accurately describes you and your feelings. Select "b" if the statement does not accurately describe you and your feelings.

If asked to describe my personality to someone I'd never met, I would use words like:

    1. a community organizer   a. Yes   b. No

    2. confident   a. Yes   b. No

    3. mature   a. Yes   b. No

    4. critical of others   a. Yes   b. No

    5. proud of my culture   a. Yes   b. No

    6. easily bored   a. Yes   b. No

Africa is a dark continent filled with hunger, poverty, and ignorance.

        a. True   b. False

I can list five living African American men that are doing positive things in their families, businesses, churches, communities, or some other organization.

        a. Yes   b. No

List them below.

    1. _____

    2. _____

    3. _____

    4. _____

    5. _____

Select the one that is most important to you. Choose only one!

        a. Being popular   b. Doing well in school

Part IV

Read the following statements and choices for answers carefully. Then pick the answer that most accurately describes your feelings.

There are NO RIGHT OR WRONG ANSWERS. Choose the answer that is right for YOU.

1. When my friends have fun without me, I
   a. am happy they are having fun.
   b. don't even think about it.
   c. wish they weren't having fun without me.

2. When I hear something negative about a person, I
   a. can't wait to tell someone else.
   b. talk to the person to see how I can help.
   c. try to find out more, because it's interesting.

3. When someone says something about me that is not good but is true, I
   a. get upset.
   b. don't want to be around them anymore.
   c. listen and learn from their observations.

4. When someone makes fun of me, I
   a. get upset.
   b. am hurt.
   c. laugh with them.
   d. make a joke of it.
   e. don't like it.

5. When I am talking to someone, most of the time I look
   a. at their hands.
   b. into their eyes.
   c. at the floor.
   d. all around.

6. I make sure I am neat and clean in my appearance.
   a. never
   b. once in a while
   c. most of the time
   d. always

7. Money is important for:
   a. buying expensive clothes.
   b. building the community we live in.
   c. buying whatever I want.
   d. saving for future plans.

8. A girl becomes a woman when (select the answer that is most important to you.)
   a. she has a baby.
   b. her body becomes more developed (she has breasts.)
   c. she takes care of herself and her family.
   d. she can talk back to her mother.
   e. she has a boyfriend

9. When I do poorly on my schoolwork, I
   a. don't really care.
   b. know I tried my best.
   c. know I should try harder.
   d. know it's only because I can't do any better.
   e. know the teacher gave us work that was too hard or boring.

10. In my involvement with organizations, I
    a. like to hold a leadership position.
    b. like to work as a team.
    c. don't like doing the dirty work.
    d. often disagree with other members.

11. When I need help, I
    a. get frustrated.
    b. ask for it.
    c. try to figure it out myself.

12. I pick my friends because
    a. they look good.
    b. they are cool.
    c. they are understanding.
    d. they have something to offer me.

13. I am glad I am the race I am.
    a. Yes
    b. No

14. I chose the answer above because
    a. I am proud of my heritage.
    b. I should be glad.
    c. I study my history and culture.
    d. my friends say it's important.

15. I like my favorite music because
    a. of its rhythm for dancing.
    b. of its positive messages.
    c. of its ability to help me relax.
    d. the rappers curse and dog out the women.
    e. the videos are nice.

16. A boy becomes a man when
    a. he can handle drugs and crime.
    b. he makes a baby.
    c. he takes responsibility for his actions.
    d. he can fight well.

17. When I attend assemblies or special events, I like to sit
    a. in the middle of the auditorium.
    b. in the front of the auditorium.
    c. in the back of the auditorium.

18. When I set a goal, I
    a. expect someone to make it happen for me.
    b. plan how I will do it and make the first step.
    c. just think about it real hard.
    d. ask my friends to get me started.

19. When the teacher leaves the room, I
    a. talk.
    b. stop doing my work.
    c. look at who is being disobedient.
    d. find something quiet to do once I finish my work.

20. I like my favorite television program because
    a. it's real funny.
    b. I enjoy the action.
    c. I enjoy the "scenery" (cars, clothes, houses, etc.)
    d. it is educational.
    e. it makes me think and discuss important issues with others.

21. Learning about one's culture and heritage is very important and helps me feel good about who I am.
    a. Yes
    b. No

22. Check the attributes that make you think of beauty.
    a. light skin
    b. dark skin
    c. natural hair
    d. long hair
    e. thin shape

23. Answering these questions was
    a. very enjoyable.
    b. no big deal.
    c. a good way to take a closer look at my personal development.
    d. a waste of time.

24. Africa has many cities.

                a. True   b. False

25. Africa is the Motherland of Black people all over the world.

                a. True   b. False

26. Egypt, also known as Kemet (which means Land of the Blacks), is in Africa which is the cradle of civilization.

                a. True   b. False

27. African people have always resisted domination all over the world.

                a. True   b. False

28. Africa is mostly jungle.

                a. True   b. False

29. Tarzan movies show you what Africa is like and used to be like.

a. True   b. False

30. Africa is a continent on which there is a cultural unity more important than the differences we hear about in the news.

a. True   b. False

Using the definitions on the right, place the corresonding letter in the space provided that you feel best fits each of the seven principles listed (Nguzo Saba).

___ 31. UMOJA

a. to build our stores and businesses to profit from them together.

___ 32. KUJICHAGULIA

b. to have a collective goal of building and developing our community.

___ 33. UJIMA

c. being creative in the way we make our communities better all the time.

___ 34. UJAMAA

d. being determined to speak up for myself.

___ 35. NIA

e. to work on challenges collectively and feel responsible as a group.

___ 36. KUUMBA

f. to believe in ourselves and that we will do great things.

___ 37. IMANI

g. to keep in touch with and offer support to friends, neighbors, and community.

HARAMBEE TIME # 1

What is SETCLAE?

> *"The journey of a thousand miles begins with one step."*
> African Proverb

WHAT DOES THIS PROVERB MEAN TO YOU?

MATERIALS: *To Be Popular or Smart: The Black Peer Group*
Lessons From History, Jr./Sr. High Edition
Miseducation of the Negro

OBJECTIVE: To examine the acronym SETCLAE and be able to clearly define the concepts of self-esteem, culture, and academic excellence as well as their relationship to each other.

WHAT IS SETCLAE?

–1a–SETCLAE is an acronym that stands for:

Self-Esteem Through Culture Leads to Academic Excellence

Write your definition of self-esteem.

_____

_____

_____

Write your definition of culture.

_____

_____

_____

Write your definition of academic excellence.

_____

_____

_____

Additional definitions of self-esteem:

- how you feel about yourself.
- the way you see yourself in terms of strengths and weaknesses, goals, personality, and values.
- to possess a favorable opinion of oneself.
- a feeling of self-respect.
- a sense of identity.
- a sense of purpose.
- a sense of personal competence.
- one of the most important possessions a person can have.

Additional definitions of culture:

- the way we speak, clothing, foods, holidays and the ways we celebrate them, religious practices.
- the vehicle which moves all human groups forward.
- the intentions, decisions, inclinations, and adjustments to life of a people who are identified as one group by blood and lineage, history and circumstance.
- a total life pattern involving the spiritual, historical, social, economic, political, creative, and psychological aspects.

Some other definitions of academic excellence:

- doing your best.
- demonstrating your highest levels of competence.
- learning to build one's sense of identity, purpose, and direction.

–1b–Discussion:

Why is culture-based curriculum important? (Read p. 101 in *Lessons From History*).

Why are programs like SETCLAE needed for African-American students and students of all ethnic backgrounds? (Read pp. xii-xiii in *Miseducation of the Negro*.)

Culture-based Curriculum

by Harold E. Charles

In August 1920, before the membership of the Universal Negro Improvement Association, Marcus Garvey electrified the thousands of delegates to this international convention by issuing a proclamation that included the rights of students to be taught Black history in their schools. Later Dr. Carter G. Woodson revived Garvey's appeal and then instituted a Negro History Week celebration in February that now has been popularized as Black History Month.

As a result of these great heroes and others, the teaching of Black heritage and culture became institutionalized in predominantly Black schools, colleges and universities throughout the South and parts of the North as well. Since then, there has been considerable agitation for widespread implementation of this concept.

Over the years, this sense of cultural and academic excellence has become diminished and mediocrity has become allowed to flourish in our community schools.

The reasons are very clear, especially when one examines the curriculum in public schools. If the lessons are not overtly racist, they oftentimes use the accomplishments of European people at the expense of offering positive images of other ethnic groups, particularly Black achievements, past and present. This is why there is a national movement to correct the textbooks and instructional material used in classrooms across the country.

We must now insist that public schools infuse a multicultural curriculum which places African and African American history in its proper context in every subject and grade level. This is why the school improvement plan must incorporate an African-centered curriculum to build student self-esteem.

Once our children are imbued with the educational foundation of cultural and academic excellence, they will then believe enough in their innate genius and creativity to aspire continually towards higher goals of achievement. Parents and educators alike have a joint responsibility to continue our quest for Afrocentrism throughout the public school curriculum.

Excerpts from the article "Culture Based Curriculum" written by Harold E. Charles

Which picture(s) best represent

SELF-ESTEEM?

CULTURE?

ACADEMIC EXCELLENCE?

And Why?

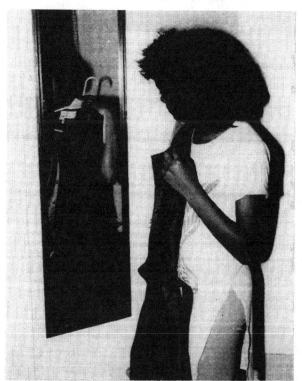

AFRICA'S CHILDREN

HARAMBEE TIME # 2

BONDING (Forming Harambee Circles)

> *"Cross the river in a crowd and the crocodile won't eat you."*
> African Proverb

WHAT DOES THIS PROVERB MEAN TO YOU?

MATERIALS

Lessons From History
College catalogues
Encyclopedias
Black Enterprise magazines

OBJECTIVE:

To provide opportunities for people to get to know each other, work together, and enjoy doing so.

To promote UMOJA (unity) and UJIMA (collective work and responsibility).

FIRST THINGS FIRST!!!

On an index card, write your name, class name, two things you like about yourself, something you do well (a talent or skill), an Adinkra symbol that exemplifies your personality(refer to the symbols found on pp. 70-71 in the SETCLAE book *Shining Legacy*), and anything else the teacher requests.

These I.D. cards will be placed in a container labeled "WA ON GOZI KWA KESHO" which means "Leaders of Tomorrow" in Kiswahili. Decorate your container with positive phrases, illustrations, and other creations.

–2a–COMPLETE THE FOLLOWING EXERCISE

A. criteria   F. dialect

B. acronym   G. administrator

C. institution   H. consultant

D. entrepreneur   I. expertise

You will become familiar with the words above as they are frequently used in the SETCLAE program. Using this word list, place the letter you feel best fits the definition on the provided line.

TRY IT FOR THREE MINUTES ONLY!

1.____ one who gives advice or opinions on a particular subject.

2.____ a variation of a particular language.

3.____ one who manages a business or institution.

4.____ standards on which a judgement may be made.

5.____ one who organizes and assumes responsibility for a business.

6.____ the skill of an expert.

7.____ a word formed from the initial letters of a group of words.

8.____ an organization for the promotion of a cause or common goal among its members.

Now try to complete the task working in your Harambee group for three minutes only.

–2b–DISCUSSION ACTIVITY

List the benefits of working in small groups.

1._____

_____

2._____

_____

3._____

_____

–2c–FORMING HARAMBEE GROUPS

HARAMBEE is a Kiswahili word meaning "Let's Pull Together!" Working in your newly formed Harambee circle, select a name for the group from the assigned category.

Group # 1 - THE **NGUZO SABA** (SEVEN PRINCIPLES)
{See p. 80 in *Lessons From History* for more info.}

UMOJA - Unity

KUJICHAGULIA - Self-Determination

UJIMA - Collective Work and Responsibility

UJAMAA - Cooperative Economics

NIA - Purpose

KUUMBA - Creativity

IMANI - Faith

Cooperative learning creates positive peer group interaction.

Group # 2 - AFRICAN COUNTRIES

NIGERIA - This West African nation is Africa's most populated country. It is rich with oil. Nigeria has six universities that provide education for over 20,000 students. Lagos is the capital city.

KENYA - This beautiful East African country is home for the Kikuyu community. Jomo Kenyatta and the Mau Mau led them to independence from the British. Nairobi is the capital city.

EGYPT - The zenith of civilization, home of the pyramids, temples, tombs, and the Sphinx. It was originally called Kemet by its inhabitants which means "Land of the Blacks".

AZANIA - Sometimes called South Africa, the name Azania is widely used by African nationalists. It is a country filled with gold and diamonds. We all must work to remove apartheid, a form of slavery. Azania means "Land of the Blacks" and promotes unity of all communities in the country.

TANZANIA - An East African country, home of the Masai community. Home of the great leader and former President Julius Nyerere who promoted self-reliance and cooperative economics through the establishment of Ujamaa villages. Dar es Salaam is the capital city.

Group # 3 - AFRICAN COMMUNITIES {See the book *Ashanti to Zulu* for more info.}

ASHANTI - Community in Ghana that weaves royal kente cloth. When Ghana was an empire, powerful kings controlled the gold in this West African community.

HENRIETTA SPEARMAN/Staff

Jomandi Productions, a living institution.

The internationally known Jubilee Singers are shown entering Fisk Memorial Chapel of Fisk University. Fisk University

YORUBA - Community in Nigeria in which there are many great artisans and craftspersons. There is a Yoruba community called Oyotunji Village in Beaufort, South Carolina. Religious aspects of The Yoruba community are practiced throughout America and the Caribbean.

CHAGGA - A community that believes in the rites of passage in which teens are prepared for adulthood.

DOGON - Community in Mali, West Africa in which the world's greatest astronomers are found. They shocked the Western scientific community with knowledge of a star called "Sirius B" because this star can not be seen with the naked eye.

ZULU - Community in Azania known for its warriors and musicians. They achieved a military victory that was the greatest defeat against the British in the late 19th century.

Group #4 - HISTORICAL AFRICAN AMERICAN COLLEGES

HAMPTON UNIVERSITY - A coed college in Hampton, Va., founded in 1868 with nearly 4500 students. The campus has its own radio and TV stations and has a lake on the campus.

FISK UNIVERSITY - Founded in 1866, Fisk is located in Nashville, Tenn. The institution is known for the Fisk Jubilee Singers, a choir that has played for kings, queens, and presidents in many parts of the world.

CLARK / ATLANTA UNIVERSITY - A merger in 1988 brought two historic institutions together. It is part of the Atlanta University Complex in Atlanta, Ga., and offers many undergraduate as well as graduate degrees (Masters' and Ph.D.'s) to its students. The school's radio station is popular throughout the city for its jazz and informative programs.

TUSKEGEE INSTITUTE - Founded by Booker T. Washington, Tuskegee is in Alabama and has nearly 3500 students. Tuskegee has a nursing program and a pre-veterinarian program.

HOWARD UNIVERSITY - Founded in Washington, D.C., in 1867, Howard is one of the largest Black colleges in the country. Howard has over 75 different majors including business, education, and advertising.

Group # 5 - INSTITUTIONS

SCIENTISTS - As a group of scientists, this institution can provide the community with information regarding diet, consumer products, new technology and can manufacture products as well.

FINANCIAL CONSULTANTS - Members of this institution can assist you with your accounting, banking, and budgeting needs.

CULTURAL ARTISTS - This institution includes writers, poets, storytellers, actors and actresses, musicians, visual artists, and dancers.

EDUCATORS - This group includes, classroom teachers, administrators, curriculum writers, college professors, consultants, and founders of independent schools and community centers.

COMMUNITY ACTIVISTS - This group includes anyone who is actively involved in the happenings and development of the community. Examples are PTA President or general member, a holder of a political office, journalists, rap artists with an educational message, and public speakers.

Group # 5 may create a name for their institution or use one of the generic names listed above.

HARAMBEE TIME # 3

Names We Call Ourselves: The Question of Identity

> *"Wood may remain ten years in the water,*
> *but will never become a crocodile."*
> *African Proverb*

MATERIALS:

Lessons From History
Developing Positive Images

OBJECTIVE:

To gather an understanding that all people belong to an ethnic group and to be able to identify one's own and others' national origin.

To appreciate the unique physical characteristics of all ethnic groups with emphasis on the fact that African Americans are many different complexions; all beautiful in their own way.

Names We Call Ourselves - The Identity Question

Use the following information to develop your own ideas on "WHO AM I?" through poetry, song, short story, essay, rap, visual depictions, etc.

Afro-American Fragment

by Langston Hughes

So long,
So far away
Is Africa.
Not even memories alive
Save those that history books create,
Save those that songs
Beat back into the blood—
Beat out of blood with words sad-sung
In strange un-Negro tongue-
So long,
So far away
Is Africa.

Subdued and time-lost
Are the drums —- and yet
Through some vast mist of race
There comes this song
I do not understand,
This song of atavistic land,

Of bitter yearnings lost
Without a place—
So long,
So far away
Is Africa's
Dark face.

Negro

I am a Negro:
Black as the night is Black,
Black like the depths of my Africa.

I've been a slave:
Caesar told me to keep his door-steps clean.
I brushed the boots of Washington.

I've been a worker:
Under my hand the pyramids arose.
I made the mortar for the Woolworth Building.

I've been a singer:
All the way from Africa to Georgia
I carried my sorrow songs.
I made ragtime.

I've been a victim:
The Belgians cut off my hands in the Congo.
They lynch me still in Mississippi.

I am a Negro:
Black as the night is black,
Black like the depths of my Africa.

> *"The Rev. Jackson announced that Americans of African descent are African-American, not 'black.' This public declaration of identity has inspired more and more African-Americans to refer to themselves accordingly."*

[The poems above can be found in *Selected Poems of Langston Hughes*, 1959, Vintage Books, New York]

A people without their culture are a people without meaning.
A people without their culture are a people without substance.
A people without their culture are a people without identity, purpose and direction.
A people without their culture are a dead people.

[Taken from *Book of Life* by Haki Madhubuti, 1973, Broadside Press, Detroit. p. 63]

"History is a clock that people use to tell their time of day. It is a compass they use to find themselves on the map of human geography. It tells them where they are, and what they are."

- John Henrik Clarke

"I am not tragically colored. There is no great sorrow damned up in my soul, nor lurking behind my eyes. I do not mind at all...I do not weep at the world-I am too busy sharpening my oyster knife."

- Zora Neale Hurston

"If you have no confidence in self you are twice defeated in the race of life. With confidence you have won even before you have started."

- Marcus Garvey

[The above quotations are taken from *Famous Black Quotations* by Janet Cheatham Bell 1986, Sabayt Publications]

PD: CHRIS STEPHENS

Kenneth Zakee of Atlanta raises the African unity Flag at the anti-drug cultural festival in the King-Kennedy public housing complex.

Were you aware of the following five benefits of having dark skin?

1. It provides protection from sunburn.

2. There is less chance of contracting skin cancer.

3. It delays the aging process.

4. The darker the skin the greater the amount of melanin in the system. The greater the amount of melanin in the system, the more the body absorbs the sun which is crucial to the production of Vitamin D. Vitamin D is crucial to the development of brain cells. Melanin has also been found to be a primary component in the creation and maintenance of the human race.

5. There is no worry or expense to get a suntan.

[See "The Mysteries of Melanin" in *From the Browder File*, by Anthony T. Browder, 1989, The Institute of Karmic Guidance, Washington, D.C. pp.91-95]

–3a–USE THE FOLLOWING FORMAT OR YOUR OWN ADAPTATION TO WRITE A POEM.

I am (your name, name of ethnic group).

I was born in (city, state, country).

I live in (city, state).

My ancestors lived in (country or continent).

I am / have (2 words describing physical appearance).

I am (3 words describing positive things about yourself).

I can (something you do well).

One day, I will (a long-term goal).

I am (your name, name of ethnic group).

Use the following materials to increase your understanding of identity as it relates to African Americans.

Lessons From History, pp. (v), 20, 87-88,

Developing Positive Images, pp. 16-17, 25-26

To Be Popular or Smart, pp. 11-32, 38.

Miseducation of the Negro, pp. 132-156.

Chains and Images of Psychological Slavery, pp. 23-26, 35-40.

–3b–"NAMES WE CALL OURSELVES"

There is a steady increase in the number of African Americans changing their names and giving their children African names as a sign of KUJICHAGULIA. {Self-determination - To define ourselves, name ourselves, and speak for ourselves instead of being named, and created for and by others.}

HARAMBEE!!! - Work in Harambee groups.

Selecting from the following names, create a skit in which each member of the group takes on one of the names listed below and explains why they chose that name. Suggestions for settings include:

> a college campus
> a community center
> a family scene
> birth of a child (naming ceremony)
> a rites-of-passage ritual (see *Countering the Conspiracy II*, pp. 43-46 and *Conspiracy III*, pp.57-65 for more info.)

Skits should be no longer than seven minutes.

Use your KUUMBA (creativity) and feel free to use songs, jokes, dances, visuals, audience participation, etc.

Refer to the book *Jomo* for additional ideas.

NAME	SEX	PRONUNCIATION	MEANING	ORIGIN / LANGUAGE
Jawanza	M	ja WAN zah	dependable	Swahili
Folami	F/M	faw LAH mee	respect and honor me	Yoruba
Rafiki	F/M	ra FEE kee	friend	Swahili
Aisha	F	ah EE shah	beautiful flower	Arabic
Babatunde	M	bah bah TOON day	father returns	Yoruba
Khalfani	M	kahl FAH nee	destined to rule	Swahili
Zakiya	F	zah Kee yah	intelligent	Swahili
Rukiya	F	roo KEE yah	she rises on high	Swahili
Sharifa	F	shah REE fah	distinguished	Swahili
Omari	M	oh MAH ree	the highest	Swahili
Jabari	M	jah BAH ree	brave	Swahili
Kamau	M	kah MAH oo	quiet warrior	Kikuyu
Ade	M	ah DAY	royal / crown	Yoruba
Talibah	F	tah LEE bah	seeker after knowledge	Arabic
Nzinga	F	N zing GAH	unconquerable queen	Angola
Rashida	F	rah SHEE dah	righteous	Arabic
Lateefah	F	lah TEE fah	gentle, pleasant	Arabic

Additional names can be found in *Golden Names for an African People*.

"Nappy:" More Than Just a Pretty Face

By Caprece Ann Jackson

For many of us, the word "nappy" conjures up negative thoughts like the clash of heat or a chemical straightener on tender scalps during childhood. Biased beauty standards have etched self-hatred into our subconscious with

the help of television and magazines. A hair industry designed to exclude grooming techniques for the natural hair of African descendants continues to snarl the psyche of African-Americans, as it has for centuries. With the 90s nipping at our heels, the dawn of an era of consciousness in the air, and the 21st century ten paces away, "Nappy" has arrived with a conscious-raising smile.

Watching "Nappy" ignite conscious-ness during festivals, bazaars and fairs in Washington, DC; Harlem and Brooklyn, NY is the propelling spark of the "Happy I'm Nappy" (H.I.N.) concept. Reversing the negative connotation associated with 'nappy' hair is the ultimate objective behind that pretty face.

The seed for the H.I.N. concept and the creation of "Nappy" was planted in 1984. When I relocated to Washington, DC from Paris, France, where I lived, wrote, and modelled professionally for five years, it never occurred to me that the option to express both sides of my bi-cultural heritage would become a priority in my life. My tiny, shoulder-length individual braids got less than an enthusiastic reception on numerous social and professional occasions. The popularity of the "curl" was at its peak. Naturals were considered passe by the masses. Most people viewed locks as a wearable plague.

When I laid eyes on the mane of natural hair worn by H.I.N. co-founder Pamela Michele "Alema" Johnson in April, 1984, my immediate thought was a question. "I wonder whether people are reacting to her, like they are reacting to me?" Alema is a Howard University graduate, born in Norfolk, VA. She and I began to converse daily about the issues that affect African-Americans who choose to express their cultural heritage by wearing natural hairstyles—braids, locks, twists and naturals.

Nappy continues to evolve. Now she is a full-body entity. Her progressive, culturally-aware perspective and effervescent character are more visible. She wears several hairstyles including the "BLT"—Braids, Locks and Twists—as well as her famous sculptured natural.

No wonder Nappy loves being nappy. The versatility of African hair surpasses that of everyone else on Earth because we can change its texture at will. Each strand has a built-in supply of 'mousse.'

Enhance your perspective by seeking knowledge about the African dimension of our multi-cultural heritage and its majestic diversity...and you will be happy you're nappy, too.

Please note: *Good hair is healthy hair.* Look for more of Nappy and Madu and new developments at Nappy Collectibles in upcoming issues of *Talking Drums.* Your comments and requests are welcome.

Excerpts from the article "Nappy: More Than Just a Pretty Face",
written by Caprece Ann Jackson - Talking Drums / March/April 1990

What images come to your mind when you hear the word nappy?

What have been the strongest influences on your perceptions of hair?

What inspires Caprece Ann Jackson to build her "Happy I'm Nappy" business?

(Items include tote bags, buttons, t-shirts, and dolls.)

HARAMBEE TIME # 4

Lessons From History

> *"History is a clock that people use to tell their time of day.
> It is a compass they use to find themselves on the map of geography.
> It tells them where they are and what they are."*
>
> Dr. John Henrik Clarke

MATERIALS: *Lessons From History*
Local and community newspapers

OBJECTIVE: To understand that history is relevant; that it teaches us lessons so that we will not repeat the same mistakes and will build on proven strengths.

To help you realize that you are a part of history and that history is made every day.

LESSONS FROM HISTORY

Let's see how and why history is relevant to our lives.

Write your definition for relevance here.

_____

_____

Read p. 97 in *Lessons From History*.

What is a lesson you can learn from history?

The pictures above capture a very important time in our history.

Left - what makes these important leaders different? What bonds them?

Use one of the "lessons from history" on the pages listed below (or one of your own) to address a current issue. Present your analytical suggestions as a song, skit, poem, picture, chart, how-to guide, fact sheet, rap, or other creative format.

Use pictures and information from local publications.

--4a--SUGGESTED AREAS--[See Lessons From History...]

p. 100 - Community Development

p. 104 - Following the messenger and not the message

p. 104-106 - African American Business Development

p. 107 - High Drop-Out Rate

p. 108 - Drug Abuse, Youth Development

Display your works on a bulletin board.

Submit them to school and community newspapers and magazines.

What lessons from history can we learn to avoid such tragedies in the future?

--4b--

A lawyer and a political leader

Nelson R. Mandela opened the first black law partnership in South Africa in 1952 in Johannesburg.

Some important dates in the life of Nelson R. Mandela:

July 18, 1918 — Nelson R. Mandela is born in Qunu, a small town in the southeastern Xhosa-speaking region of Transkei, the son of a Tembu tribal leader.

1938 — Mr. Mandela enters the University of Fort Hare. Two years later, he is expelled for participating in a student strike and moves to Johannesburg to avoid an arranged marriage.

1941 — He completes work for his bachelor's degree by correspondence and studies law at the University of the Witwatersrand in Johannesburg.

1944 — He, Oliver Tambo and Walter Sisulu help form the Youth League of the African National Congress.

1948 — Mr. Mandela becomes national secretary of the ANC Youth League. In 1950, he becomes its president.

1952 — Mr. Mandela is appointed "volunteer-in-chief" of the ANC's Defiance Campaign and travels around the country recruiting volunteers prepared to break apartheid laws.

June 26, 1952 — The Defiance Campaign opens. Mr. Mandela and 51 others break curfew regulations as their first act of defiance.

December 1952 — Mr. Mandela and Mr. Tambo open a law practice in Johannesburg, the first black law partnership in the country. In the same month, Mr. Mandela and others are arrested and charged under the Suppression of Communism Act. He receives a suspended prison sentence and is prohibited from attending meetings or leaving Johannesburg.

September 1953 — Mr. Mandela's restrictions are renewed, and he is required to resign officially from the ANC. Thereafter, his leadership role is exercised secretly.

Dec. 6, 1956 — Mr. Mandela is among 156 political leaders arrested and charged with high

June 1958 — Mr. Mandela marries Winnie Nomzamo Madikizela, a social worker, after divorcing his first wife, Evelyn.

March 21, 1960 — Sixty-nine black protesters are killed by police in Sharpeville. A state of emergency is declared, and the ANC is outlawed.

March 29, 1961 — Mr. Mandela and all his co-defendants in the treason case are acquitted after a 4½-year trial. He helped conduct the defense. For the next 17 months, he lives as a fugitive and becomes commander of the ANC's newly formed military wing, Umkhonto we Sizwe (Spear of the Nation).

Jan. 11, 1962 — After being smuggled across the border, Mr. Mandela makes a surprise appearance at the Pan-African Freedom Movement Conference in Ethiopia. He then travels to Algeria for guerrilla training and to London to meet leftist politicians.

Aug. 5, 1962 — A few weeks after returning to South Africa, he is captured and charged with incitement and leaving the country illegally.

November 1962 — He is convicted and sentenced to five years in prison.

July 11, 1963 — While Mr. Mandela is in prison, police raid the ANC's underground headquarters at a farmhouse in Rivonia, outside Johannesburg, and seize documents outlining a planned guerrilla campaign.

Oct. 20, 1963 — The so-called Rivonia Trial of Mr. Mandela and eight co-defendants begins. They are accused of sabotage and conspiracy to overthrow the government.

April 20, 1964 — As the trial nears its end, Mr. Mandela gives his famous statement from the dock. He explains the ANC's shift to violence after six decades as a non-violent organization and says he is prepared to die for the ideal of a democratic South Africa.

June 12, 1964 — Eight of the nine accused, including Mr. Mandela, receive life sentences.

May 12, 1984 — Mr. Mandela and his wife are allowed their first contact visit and embrace for the first time in 22 years.

Jan. 31, 1985 — President P.W. Botha offers to free Mr. Mandela if he renounces violence. Mr. Mandela says he will not do so until the government takes the initiative in dismantling apartheid and granting full political rights to blacks.

July 18, 1988 — Mr. Mandela's 70th birthday is observed by anti-apartheid activists worldwide. Most public commemorations in South Africa are banned.

Aug. 12, 1988 — Mr. Mandela is hospitalized for tuberculosis.

Dec. 6, 1988 — After recovery, Mr. Mandela is transferred to Victor Verster prison farm in Paarl, north of Cape Town, where he lives in a house and is allowed unrestricted family visits.

Feb. 16, 1989 — Leading anti-apartheid groups repudiate Winnie Mandela, accusing her of complicity in the abduction and assault of a 14-year-old black activist and of letting her bodyguards wage a "reign of terror" in Soweto. Some of the bodyguards are charged with the boy's murder.

May 17, 1989 — Mr. Mandela receives his bachelor of laws degree, which he earned through correspondence study with the University of South Africa.

July 5, 1989 — Mr. Botha invites Mr. Mandela to his official Cape Town residence for a 45-minute talk.

Oct. 15, 1989 — Mr. Sisulu and four other co-defendants of Mr. Mandela are freed unconditionally by Frederik W. de Klerk, who replaced Mr. Botha as president in August.

Dec. 13, 1989 — Mr. Mandela confers with Mr. de Klerk at the presidential office in Cape Town.

Feb. 2, 1990 — Mr. de Klerk legalizes the ANC and 60 other organizations, vows to free all political prisoners, ends restrictions on 374 individuals and places a moratorium on hangings.

Feb. 10, 1990 — Mr. de Klerk announces that Mr. Mandela will be released from prison the next day.

Feb. 11, 1990 — Mr. Mandela leaves prison.

Source: The Associated Press

What lessons can we learn from the history of Nelson Mandela and his people's fight to abolish apartheid?

HARAMBEE TIME # 5

Africa: The Cradle of Civilization

> *"Through recent anthropological discoveries, science has substantially established that the cradle of humanity is Africa.*
> *For the American Negro there is a special relationship with Africa.*
> *It is the land of his origin. It was despoiled by invaders;*
> *its culture was arrested and concealed to justify white supremacy.*
> *The American Negro's ancestors were not only driven into slavery,*
> *but their links with their past were severed so that*
> *their servitude might be psychological as well as physical."*
>
> Rev. Dr. Martin Luther King, Jr.

MATERIALS:

Lessons From History
Budweiser Poster Series - African Kings and Queens
Additional materials depicting Africa as the cradle of civilization

OBJECTIVE:

To increase your knowledge of ancient and contemporary Africa.

To increase your knowledge of Egypt with a clear understanding that Egypt is a country in Africa, that it is the zenith of civilization, and that ancient Egyptians were African people.

AFRICA, THE CRADLE OF CIVILIZATION

National Museum Of Zimbabwe in downton Harare.

This auction block is located on Goree Island, a small island off the coast of Senagal in west Africa. 20 millions slaves were shipped through Goree to the Americas during the slave trade. Three million died in dungeons here while another six million died at sea. A visit to Goree is a popular and often emotional trip for African-American tourists.

Photo by Shaka Kusadi

Queens Of The Nile On Parade

Scene from "Queens of the Nile, Now" Royal Family Dinner Show produced by the Queens Historical Society and sponsored by Budweiser Beer.

Togo, a tiny country adjacent to Ghana, is very beautiful and modern in many ways, yet it has the rural African mistique that visitors love. This round building (above) in the capitol city of Lome is an example of some of the spectacular sites that have resulted from Togo's recent wave of development.

WRITING ACTIVITY

What words and images come to your mind when you hear the word Africa?

Where have you learned what you know about Africa?

–5a–HARAMBEE!

(Work in Harambee circles.)

Lessons From History, pp. 1-10

pp. 5(b-e) in this workbook

Develop a rap, skit, poem, story, and/or illustration that presents information in the category assigned to your group. Your group presentation should be no longer than 3 minutes.

1. Geographical facts about Africa

2. African kings and queens

3. Egypt is in Africa!!!

4. Science, education, and architecture in ancient Africa

5. Empires and religion in Africa

JUST FOR FUN

Between presentations, use the following chants as the next group takes the stage.

I don't want my history
to be no mystery
to me.

I didn't know before
And now I know more
about Egypt.

Egypt is in Africa!
Egypt is in Africa!

MAKE UP YOUR OWN!

–5b–Shining the Light in Hieroglyphs

Hieroglyphs were created by a great African civilization. It is a form of picture writing developed by the ancient Egyptians. People who were taught to read and to use hieroglyphs were called scribes. Children studying to be scribes had to learn more than 700 different signs and put them together in the right way.

Some hieroglyphs represent sounds, while others represent objects or ideas. You can use hieroglyphs as a code language by swapping the single letters of the Egyptian alphabet for the English letters. Some of the English letters are missing from this alphabet, like E and O. However, the Egyptians themselves mostly did without the vowels AEIOU altogether, and you can do the same.

Include the activity on p. 20 in *Color Me Light of the World* - p. 20

–5c–Egypt is in Africa!

Select an Egyptian in history and memorize his/her story. Get a family member to help you by looking at the words while you speak from memory. When you have memorized it well, read it to everyone in your house.

Design something you can wear, carry, or display when you speak to the class as this leader (for example, a crown, a picture of a pyramid). Use other books, magazines, and encyclopedias for ideas.

Imhotep

I am Imhotep. I am an ancient African. I lived in ancient Egypt in the Third Dynasty which was around 2,700 years before Christ. I was the builder and planner (planned the building) for the first Step Pyramid for the Pharaoh Zozer (Z0-sher).

I was also the first doctor. I lived 2,000 years before Hippocrates the Greek. The Europeans call him the Father of Medicine, but I came before him and I was called the "God of Medicine."

Queen Nefertari

I am Queen Nefertari (Ne-Fer-tah-ree) of the 18th Dynasty of Egypt. I am one of the great Black queens of Egypt. I was very active in the participation and leadership in national affairs. My son was Amenhotep I and my husband was Ahmose.

Queen Hatshepsut

I am Queen Hatshepsut. I had a very brilliant mind, which I used to build Egypt. I did such things as expand foreign trade, build a navy, and develop public buildings. I was also a Pharaoh.

Some say I was the greatest ruler of all time.

Akhenaten

I am King Akhenaten, Pharaoh of the 18th Dynasty. I am the father of the "Trinity of God" concept which was copied by others.

I was called the champion of "peace on earth and goodwill towards men" over 1,000 years before the birth of Christ.

My name is also Amen-hotep IV.

Piankhy

I am Pharaoh Piankhy of about 720 years before Christ. I am an Ethiopian king who conquered and ruled Egypt. My conquest of Egypt was brilliantly done. My story is told on a granite stele (STA-le) which is a tablet of stone that has on its four sides the story of my victory over Egypt.

Tutankhamen

I am Pharoah Tutankhamen. You know me as King Tut. I am Black. I lived long ago in the 18th Dynasty. They called me the Boy King. The gold-loving Europeans invaded my tomb and took the beautiful jewels and carvings which were placed there. Millions of people line up to see me, but they are not told that I was Black and that I come from an African culture.

−5d−AFRICA, THE CRADLE OF CIVILIZATION

Pick a country and gather information using current news articles, interviews with people who have lived there, and correspondence with embassies and pen pals.

MAP OF AFRICA - Worksheet 11 in SETCLAE grades 3-5

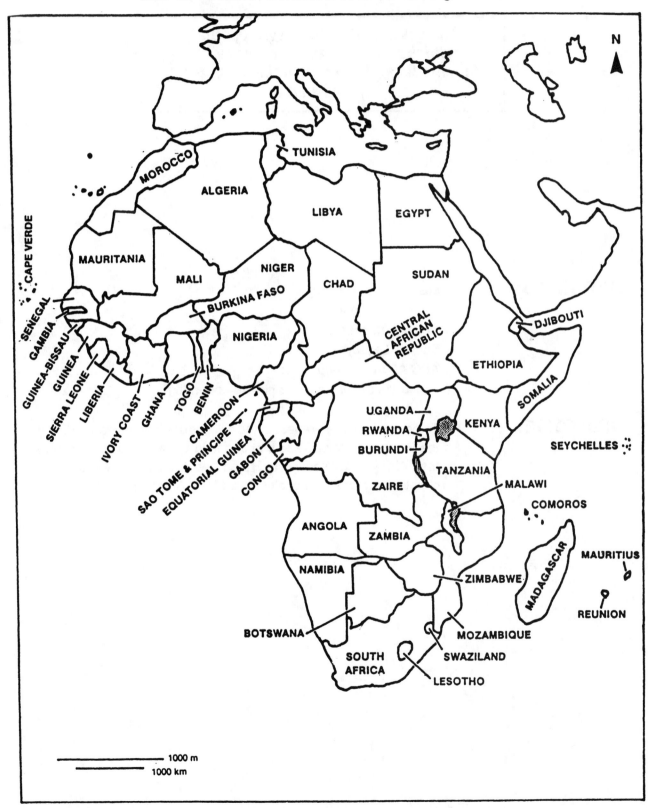

HARAMBEE TIME # 6

The Middle Passage: The African Holocaust

> *"There is a debt to the Negro people*
> *which America can never repay.*
> *At least then, they must make amends."*
> *Sojourner Truth*

MATERIALS:

Lessons From History
Construction paper
Coloring materials
Shining Legacy
ABC Africa Coloring Book
  (use illustrations as your picture appendix)

OBJECTIVE:

To increase your awareness of the millions of African lives lost during the European Slave Trade that began in 1444 and lasted for more than 400 years. Working in Harambee circles, you will produce chapters comprising a book entitled "The African Holocaust."

THE AFRICAN HOLOCAUST

–6a–WRITING ACTIVITY

What does the word holocaust mean?_____

Does anyone know what is meant by "The Middle Passage"?_____

> During the European Slave Trade, Africa lost an estimated one hundred million people. In his book, <u>Before the Mayflower,</u> Lerone Bennett states that "the slave trade was a Black man who stepped out of his hut for a breath of fresh air and ended up, ten months later, in Georgia with bruises on his back and a brand on his chest... The slave trade was a Black mother suffocating her newborn baby because she didn't want him to grow up a slave...The slave trade was a greedy king raiding his own villages to get slaves to buy brandy....The slave trade was deserted villages, bleached bones on slave trails and people with no last names."

Do these series of historical events fit the criteria for a holocaust?

Do you think Africans resisted the conditions imposed on them in the Middle Passage? How? (See *Lessons*, pp. 24-26 for examples}

What are some of the reasons we may not be as familiar with the occurrences of the African Holocaust as we are with the Jewish Holocaust?

Can anyone name another holocaust in history?

How do you think a holocaust might affect the self-esteem of its victims?

Why is it important to be aware of and remember these holocausts?

HARAMBEE!

Working in Harambee groups, design one to four pages to be included in a book entitled "The African Holocaust". Your group's contribution is the only one covering that historical era. Make it interesting so that even those that don't normally like to read will find it eye-catching. Make sure it appeals to the middle and high school student.

ALL CIRCLES ARE TO USE PICTURES TO ADD VISUALS TO THEIR CONTRIBUTION. Use the following books for more information and ideas:

Lessons From History (see page listings under each category)
Shining Legacy
ABC Africa Coloring Book

Put all the contributions together to form a book entitled "The African Holocaust." Select a classmate with artistic talents to design the cover.

Display the book in your school library / media center.

Visit other schools and community centers and share it with children of all ages.

Reproduce the book and sell it as a fundraiser.

–6b–HARAMBEE CIRCLE # 1 (The Nguzo Saba)

Your historical era is "African Capture During the European Slave Trade"

> "...The slave trade was a Black man, who stepped out of his hut for a breath of fresh air and ended up, ten months later, in Georgia with bruises on his back and a brand on his chest..."
>
> -Lerone Bennett, *Before the Mayflower*, Penguin Books

As a group, read and review pp. 13-17 in *Lessons From History*.

Select one group member to take notes.

Develop your rendition of this period in history in one to four pages.

HARAMBEE CIRCLE # 2 (The African Country)

Your historical era is "The Middle Passage."

The following quote is the story of an African man and his experiences traveling through The Middle Passage in the 17th century.

> "At the time we came into this ship, she was full of Black people, who were all confined in a dark and low place, in irons. The women were in irons as well as the men. When they put us in irons to be sent to our place of confinement in the ship, the men who fastened the irons on these mothers took the children out of their hands and threw them over the side of the ship into the water. When this was done, two of the women leaped overboard after the children - the third was already confined by a chain to another woman and could

not get into the water, but in a struggle to disengage herself, she broke her arm and died a few days after of a fever...We had nothing to eat but yams which were thrown amongst us at random... More than one-third of us died on the passage and when we arrived at Charleston, I was not able to stand...I have been here for five years."

-*Julius Lester,* To Be A Slave, pp. 25-27, Scholastic Books,1968.

As a group, read and review pp. 17-19 in *Lessons From History*.

Develop your rendition of this historical period for the history book in one to four pages.

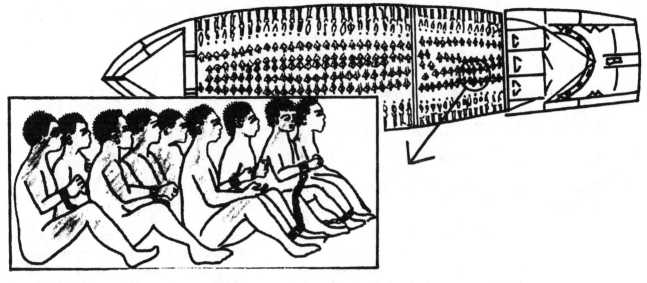

HARAMBEE CIRCLE # 3 (The African Community)

Your historical era is "The Enslavement of Africans."

The following poem is written by Phillis Wheatley, an enslaved African "bought" in 1761 by Susannah Wheatley who was the wife of a Boston merchant. Phillis was only seven years old when she arrived in Boston and was named for the ship that brought her to slavery. At the age of nineteen, her first and only book of poetry was published. The book, entitled *Poems on Various Subjects, Religious and Moral,* was the 2nd book published by an American woman and the first ever published by an African American of either sex. Her popularity as a poet among the English, Scottish, and Bostonians eventually led Ms. Wheatley to her freedom somewhere between 1773 and 1774.

"Should you, my lord, while you peruse my song,
Wonder from whence my love of freedom sprung,
Whence flow these wishes for the common good,
Be feeling hearts alone best understood,

I, young in life, by seeming cruel fate
Was snatch'd from Afric's fancied happy seat:
What pangs excruciating must molest,
What sorrows labour in my parent's breast?
Steeled was that soul and by no misery moved,
That from a father seized his babe beloved:
Such, such my case. And can I then but pray
Others may never feel tyrannic sway?

- Taken from Phillis Wheatley *by Merel Richmond, Chelsea House, NY, 1988*

Read and review pp. 19-23 in *Lessons From History*.

Select one group member to take notes.

Develop your rendition of this period in history in one to four pages.

HARAMBEE CIRCLE # 4 (Historically African American College)

Your historical era is "Resistance."

The following is an excerpt from a speech given by Sojourner Truth at a Women's Rights Convention in 1853.

" Why do I remain here, tied down a slave to work, accomplishing nothing, moving from one worry to another, getting nowhere? What has been holding me to this one spot, praying and preaching, working and slaving, and making no headway? I am meant to do greater things than these I am doing. I feels it in me...My spirit calls me to travel..I must go...I shall go...My name was Isabella; but when I left the house of bondage, I left everything behind...And the Lord gave me [the name] Sojourner because I was to travel up an' down the land showin' the people their sins an' the Lord give me "Truth" because I was to declare the truth to the people."

As a group, read and review pp. 25 - top of 29 in *Lessons From History*.

Select someone to take notes.

Develop your rendition of this historical era in one to four pages.

HARAMBEE CIRCLE # 5 (The Institution)

Your historical era is "Reparations."

Upon "Emancipation" in 1863, there was a great deal of debate around what should be done about the newly freed African Americans. After conferring with African leaders, General Sherman of the Union Army granted 40-acre plots to Africans on the coast of Georgia and S.C. African veterans of the Civil War began to demand 40 acres and a mule as reparations for enslavement.

 A Pennsylvania congressman named Thaddeus Stevens also proposed distribution of 40-acre plots and one mule to the "freedmen." Congress refused to consider this proposal. Other similar proposals such as provisions of homes and land were also adamantly refused.

Some African Americans are still involved in the fight for the equivalent of this 40 acres and a mule. This movement is called Reparations. (See the flyer below from a Reparations Conference held in Cleveland, Ohio in September 1990.) Christopher Alston is a reparations researcher and has accumulated many old news articles, letters, and various other documents. This historical exhibit gives historical details of the tens of thousands of African Americans involved in the demand for reparations in the late 1800s and early 1900s.

Read pp. 35 - 51 in *Lessons From History* (with emphasis on p. 35).

Select someone to take notes.

Develop your rendition of this period in history in one to four pages.

Queen Mother Moore has been involved in the fight for reparations for over 50 years. She currently lives in New York.

N'COBRA

SECOND NATIONAL CONFERENCE
REPARATIONS
IN OUR LIFETIME
AND THE FUTURE OF HOUSE BILL HR 3745

JOIN US TO DISCUSS, STRATEGIZE, AND DEMAND REPARATION PAYMENTS OWED TO AFRICAN AMERICANS, FOR THE INJUSTICE, CRUELTY, BRUTALITY, AND INHUMANITY OF SLAVERY AND DISCRIMINATION THAT STILL AFFECTS THE EVERYDAY LIFE OF AFRICAN AMERICANS TODAY.   JOIN US IN OUR CALL FOR REPARATIONS NOW!

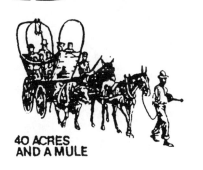

40 ACRES
AND A MULE

REPARATIONS...
YES
H.R.3745

–6c–THROUGH THE YEARS by Abiodun Oyewole

In his book *Rooted in the Soil*, Self-Published, NY,1983

Now if you don't know - four hundred years ago
Blacks were brought here as slaves
to work the land, every woman and man
and be buried in unmarked graves.
But as time moved on - and Blacks got strong
we let the world know just who we be
and it wasn't long - before they heard our song
and some died trying to be free.
But through the years - and all our fears
Black people have emerged as great
writers and doctors, farmers - and inventors
and those who helped the slaves escape.
Now there was Oliver Cromwell - who guided George Washington across the Delaware
and Lucy Terry who wrote about Custer
and how the Indians took his yellow hair
Then Joseph Cinque stole the Armistad - a shipload of slaves
to make it all the way back to Africa
through the wind and the angry waves.
Now I know about Sojourner Truth
and how she spoke out against slavery
and Nat Turner who decided to fight
and show his bravery.

Then there was Booker T. Washington
and Mary McLeod Bethune - they both started their own schools
to teach Blacks how to control their destiny
and stop being used like second hand tools.
Jan Matzeliger invented a shoe machine
to make a thousand pairs of shoes everyday.
And Benjamin Banneker was an astronomer
who read the stars in the Milky Way
Then there was Dr. Daniel Hale Williams
who started heart surgery long before anyone else
and Dr. Charles Drew - who knew what blood plasma could do

even though he couldn't save himself.
But let's not leave the music out
we've been Masters for a very long time
Stevie and Aretha can make you shout -
cause the drum stays on our minds
Bird and Diz taught us what Jazz is
and John Coltrane played a mean saxophone
Mingus and Monk kept the Juju alive
and the rhythm took us all the way home
Black history ain't no mystery
About how great Blacks have been
Black history is the epitome
of a story of a people who can win.

HARAMBEE TIME # 7

Exemplary African Excellence & Leadership

> *"Your world is as big as you make it."*
> Georgia Douglas Johnson

MATERIALS:
Lessons From History
Shining Legacy
Great Negroes Past and Present
35 index cards (7 for each Harambee circle)
Coloring materials
2 rolls of scotch tape
Current magazines and local newspapers (Ebony, Essence, Emerge, Black Enterprise, African Commentary, Jet, etc.)

OBJECTIVE:
To offer examples of excellence and leadership of Africans around the world.

To identify characteristics of yourself in these examples.

AFRICAN EXCELLENCE

"[We] are wrong,...in failing to realize that what others have done, we may not need to do. If we are to duplicate from century to century the same feats, the world will grow tired of such a monotonous performance."

- Carter G. Woodson, Miseducation of the Negro, p. 138

–7a–HARAMBEE!!!   (Work in Harambee groups.)

Gather the following materials:

> 7 index cards
> selected books from SETCLAE
> current magazines and local newspapers
> coloring materials

Use the materials above to learn about seven leaders. Use the following five categories to classify all seven leaders. You must select at least one leader from each category listed below. Examples from each category are also listed. Most examples can be found in the SETCLAE materials.

Science - Mae Jemison, Walter Massey

Education - Marva Collins, Jawanza Kunjufu, Johnetta Cole

Economic Development - Ed Gardner, John Johnson

Literature and Other Arts - Spike Lee, Chinua Achebe, Oprah Winfrey

Freedom Fighters - Sojourner Truth, Nat Turner, Winnie Mandela, Toussaint L'ouverture, Harriet Tubman

Other stipulations are:

1. At least one leader must live in a country outside of North America.

2. At least two leaders must be members of your community.

3. At least three leaders must be living.

4. At least three leaders must be women.

5. At least one leader should be under the age of 30.

6. Identify at least one leadership trait for each person in order to see how you can incorporate them into your actions, behaviors, and personalities.

–7b–NEXT!!!!

Prepare a presentation for each of the seven leaders.

The following stipulations are:

1. Each Harambee group member must present at least one of the leaders to the general body.

2. The presentation for each leader can be no longer than one minute.

3. Each Harambee group must have one presentation that uses each of the following formats:

An interview of the Leader
A rap or poem
A song or story
A TV news-style report
something visual (a photograph, poster, illustration, artifact, video, etc.)

Decorate the other side of the card with your Harambee group name and logo or make sure each Harambee group uses a different color index card and just write the name of the group on each card.

NEXT!!!!

PART II (a follow-up session)

Allow each group to present their leaders using the various categories. For example, have each group present their Living Leaders at one time or their Women or their Freedom Fighters, etc.

After all presentations, play a relay race game with each Harambee group receiving seven index cards with at least one from each Harambee group.

With each of the five categories posted on a wall or chalkboard, two teams line up to try to tape each card under the correct category. Tape each card with the Harambee group name and logo showing. When the relay race is over and card placements are being judged, allow the "producers" of that card to set the record straight.

CREATE MANY MANY VARIATIONS OF THE GAME!!!!

HARAMBEE TIME # 8

Math, Science, and Technology:
What Africa Has to Say

"The ancient Egyptians [Kemetians] did not separate or divorce the spiritual from the scientific. They employed a sacred science which produced miracles of technological achievement which still cannot be understood today."

Ramona Hodge Edelin

MATERIALS: *Lessons From History*

OBJECTIVE: To show Africa's and African American's contributions in the areas of math, science, and technology.

A PLAY

MATH, SCIENCE, AND TECHNOLOGY: WHAT AFRICA HAS TO SAY

Written by Kwesi James

{The characters are listed at the beginning of each of the seven scenes in this 2-act play.}

PROPS

bell	clock	cup
baskets	4 wooden poles	test tubes
book	easel with paper	peanuts in shell
3 tables	rattle	drum

ACT I   Past ..... Future

Scene I

CHARACTERS

MUSICIAN
NARRATOR
2 FEMALE DANCERS
2 MALE DANCERS

(Lights out)

(Music…first a bell, then drumming starting soft then getting louder and then getting softer.)

NARRATOR: In the beginning there was darkness and God said let there be light. *(Spotlight on narrator)* WELCOME, we are going to take a journey that spans thousands of years and ends in the future. We will begin at the birthplace of humankind and civilization…Africa, also called: Egypt, Kemet, Nubia, Alkebu, Ethiopia, or the Dark Continent…where women and men began to unlock the secrets and mysteries of the universe…the place where people studied nature, and nature was the first teacher, and the environment the first school. Come with us on a journey to Africa to uncover the origins of math, science, medicine, architecture, metallurgy, agriculture, numerology, physics, algebra, chemistry, geometry, astronomy, astrology, calculus, and engineering. Let's see what Africa has to say.

(Music)

(Drumming gets louder)

(Lights…go up on stage)

> *ACTION:* 8-I2 female students dance onto the stage. They kneel down in the center of the stage in rows of 2's, 3's or 4's.

(Music... stops)

NARRATOR: The Africans were the first to light the way by domesticating fire nearly one million four hundred thousand years ago. Women observing the correlation between their cycles and the cycles of the moon developed calendars and then Africans gave birth to agriculture which thus planted the seeds for civilization.

(Music)

(Drumming starts up)

> *ACTION*: Four males with long sticks dance onto stage. They dance around the females on the floor. They go down the rows imitating hoeing the soil. They go down the rows imitating planting seeds. They go down the rows imitating watering the seeds. The females raise up. The males go down the rows imitating hoeing the crop. The females stand all the way up. The males form circles around the females and dance off the stage with them.

Scene II

CHARACTERS

NARRATOR
LIBATION ORATOR
HARVEST FESTIVAL PARTICIPANTS
2 FEMALE DANCERS

NARRATOR: The Africans did not separate science from spirituality. The Africans were and are very spiritual people. They created sacred science. They acknowledged Creation in all that they did and do. They created harvest festivals to give reverence for the success of the harvest and to acknowledge Creation's role in all endeavors. These harvest festivals continue to this day throughout Africa and the world. The tradition of harvest or first-fruits festivals was called Pert-In-Min by the Egyptians or Kemetians, New Yam Festival among the Ashanti and Yoruba, Kwanzaa for African Americans, and from the American Indians we get what is now known as Thanksgiving.

These ceremonies are characterized by reverence for Creation and the ancestors, reunion of family and friends and the passing down of cultural traditions and values. Let's sit in on a harvest festival…

> *ACTION*: People come in on stage and greet each other with hugs as if they haven't seen each other for a long time. (They are dressed in all different types of ethnic clothing).

> People bring covered dishes and place them on the table. People gather around a table and sit down. Someone leads a libation pouring.

LIBATION ORATOR: In the tradition of our ancestors we pour a libation to recognize and give thanks to the Supreme Being which some people call God, Allah, Jehovah, Jah, Ausar-Auset, Amen Ra, or Oludumare. We ask that you keep illness away from our community, we ask that you keep us safe from harm and we ask that you make us prosperous people. (Pretend to pour out some liquid.) *People respond with Ase [ah-shay].* We give recognition and honor to our ancestors, those that paved the path that we now walk, we ask for your blessings, your wisdom, your strength and your assistance as we strive to add to your legacy.

(Pretend to pour out some liquid. People respond with Ase {ah-shay}.)

This we do for our future, for our seeds, our children and those yet unborn so that they will continue to honor us when we are ancestors.

(Pretend to pour out some liquid. People respond with Ase. Libation orator waves his/her hand over the food. Everyone eats.)

(Music)

(Drumming begins)

ACTION: Females come on stage with baskets and dance. People at the table join in the dance.

(Everyone exits.)

Scene III

CHARACTERS

NARRATOR
IMHOTEP
MOTHER
CHILD
*6 STUDENTS FOR PYRAMID * (See Appendix)*

NARRATOR: Did you enjoy yourselves? Very good. While I was away, I had the opportunity to meet a fascinating and remarkable person. But before I tell you about him...I would like to know by a show of hands, how many of you would like to be an architect? What about a doctor? What about a philosopher? Would anyone like to be a magician? What about a teacher? Who would like to be a politician or work in government? Would anyone like to be a poet or writer?

Well now, the person I met is named Imhotep and he is considered the world's first recorded multi-genius. He was an advisor to the king, an architect that designed and built the first step pyramid, the first father of medicine as well as a philosopher, magician, teacher, and poet. Imhotep lived in a land called Nubia thousands of years ago, let's pay him a visit...

ACTION: Imhotep is on stage drawing something at his desk. A mother and child come on stage and the child appears sickly. Imhotep talks to the mother, then checks out the patient. He shakes a rattle towards the east, north, west, and south and pretends to pick some leaves off a plant and mix them in a bowl. He then consults a book and adds more ingredients to the bowl. He gives it to the child, the child holds it up to the east, north, west, and south and then drinks it. Then Imhotep talks to the mother and she and her child exit off stage.

Imhotep then goes back to the desk and draws something. He then holds up a drawing of a step pyramid. He then goes to a group of children and directs them to form a pyramid.

{To perform optional magic trick, select a student expert.}

Then the formerly sick child returns on stage feeling better. They walk off stage in conversation.

IMHOTEP: EAT, DRINK AND BE MERRY!!!

Scene IV

(On one side of the stage, there is a Native American community. On the other side of the stage is an African community.)

CHARACTERS

NARRATOR
CHRISTOPHER COLUMBUS
AFRICAN VILLAGERS
NATIVE AMERICAN VILLAGERS

NARRATOR: Yes, "Eat, drink and be merry" is just one of the things Hippocrates stole from Imhotep. Building on the legacy of Imhotep, our ancestors developed the first civilization in Egypt (or Kemet) and reached out and brought civilization to the world.

Their genius is still awesome when one tries to comprehend the level of math, science, engineering, and architecture needed to build the great pyramids thousands of years ago: structures that are still here today. Many of these great pyramids were educational temples where the initiate (student) learned medicine, architecture, law, history, religion, astronomy, and philosophy.

In addition, the students studied the secrets and mysteries of the universe. At these great learning centers European scholars like Plato, Pythagoras, Hippocrates, Herodotus, and others were educated. The Egyptian or Kemetic spiritual and religious teachings inspired Judaism, Christianity, Islam, Hinduism, Buddhism, Yoruba, and more.

Continuing forward through time many African civilizations continued the legacy of ancient Egypt or Kemet creating great learning centers that led the world in math, science, and technology. Some of the notable cities were Timbuktu and Jenne as well as the empires of Ghana, Mali, Angola, and Great Zimbabwe.

One of the great empires or people were the Moors. The Moors were quite skilled at mathematics, numerology, astronomy, and astrology. They civilized Southern Europe and introduced colleges and libraries to the less developed Europeans. The Moors established great learning centers like Carthage and Fez in Morocco, North Africa, which has the oldest continuous college in the world today. Also, the Moors had advanced navigational technology and taught with globes while the Europeans thought that the world was flat.

> *ACTION*: Students on floor form one to three rows between the two villages. They are on their knees imitating the ocean. Then a ship leaving the Native American community with a Moorish (African) crew moves toward the African village while a ship with Columbus and African Americans sails toward the Native American village.

NARRATOR: While Christopher Columbus was sailing along the coast of West Africa, he came across Africans on their way back from the Caribbean and Central America. Columbus, assisted by the navigational expertise of the Moors, traveled to the Caribbean and never reached the American mainland.

The arrival of the European to the Americas resulted in two holocausts. The first holocaust was the virtual extinction of the Native American population. The second holocaust came with the stealing, importing, and enslaving of Africans from West, Central, and Southern Africa. Some

50

estimate as many as 100 million Africans died just in transit from Africa to the Americas. However, now the genius and light from Africa was transplanted to the Western Hemisphere.

(Dim lights)

ACT II   Future...Past

Scene V

(Set up the stage as follows):

1. Three to five students stand in a circle holding hands.
2. Table with test tubes and peanuts.
3. Table with clock, book, and easel with drawing paper.
4. One person stands with arms by his/her side.
5. Table with lamp.

CHARACTERS

NARRATOR
3-5 PEOPLE (see set-up #1)
ELIJAH MCCOY
GEORGE W. CARVER
BENJAMIN BANNEKER
GARRETT A. MORGAN
LOUIS LATIMER
One Person (see set-up #4)
2-5 PEOPLE (acting as cars)

(Spotlight on NARRATOR)

NARRATOR: Initially, the genius of the African was not documented since they often did not get patents for their inventions. However, Africans in America have contributed greatly to the technological development of the United States and the world. Let's meet a few of these great inventors, scientists, and mathematicians.

> *ACTION: The 3-5 people (set-up # 1) move their hands and arms up and down to simulate a machine.*

NARRATOR: Are you the real McCoy?

ELIJAH MCCOY: Yes, that's me. Elijah McCoy. Did you know that when people say the expression, "The Real McCoy," they are referring to <u>me</u>, Elijah McCoy, an African American inventor?

NARRATOR: No, I did not know that. Why do they call you the real McCoy?

ELIJAH MCCOY: Well, in my day, machines had to be shut down periodically in order to oil the moving parts. See! (He points to circle of 3-5 people.)

> *ACTION: They stop moving their arms. McCoy walks over to the circle and tinkers with their hands. They start moving their arms again.*

ELIJAH MCCOY: Well, thanks to my invention of an automatic lubricating device, this costly inconvenience was resolved. For a long time people wanted my device on their machines and consequently they would ask before purchasing a machine "Is it the real McCoy?"

51

NARRATOR: That's fascinating. Is there more?

ELIJAH MCCOY: Yes. I patented over twenty lubricants, an ironing board, and a lawn sprinkler.

NARRATOR: Well, thank you, Mr. McCoy. We appreciate your contributions.

ACTION: McCoy and 3-5 people in circle exit. Narrator walks toward set-up # 2.

NARRATOR: You must be George Washington Carver.

GW CARVER: *(Facing the narrator)* I certainly am, young man.

NARRATOR: What are you doing?

GW CARVER: Right now I am developing different uses for the peanut. I am up to 273 and before I finish I'll have over 350 products.

NARRATOR: WOW! Over 350 uses for the peanut! Why the peanut?

GW CARVER: I introduced crop rotation to the south. At first farmers mainly planted cotton and tobacco, which takes nitrates out of the soil. By planting legumes like peanuts and soybeans, which put nitrates back into the soil, one can increase the yield dramatically. Many farmers were storing peanuts and allowing them to rot. But, with the large number of products I've invented, the demand for peanuts has increased. Some say that I revolutionized agriculture in the South.

NARRATOR: With your talent I understand you have had many job offers including an offer of $100,000 from the Edison Company but you turned them down. Why?

GW CARVER: Yes, this is true. Before working at Tuskegee Institute, I was a faculty member at another school with many resources. However, when Booker T. Washington called on me, I answered the call. I am committed to Tuskegee Institute and my people.

NARRATOR: Where did you get such lovely paintings?

GW CARVER: I painted them, I also developed many of the dyes and paints that I use to paint... Once, one of my teachers thought that I should go to Paris to study art, but I decided against it.

NARRATOR: I'm curious. How are you able to know so much about plants?

GW CARVER: I am a humble and spiritual man. I simply take walks in the woods and the plants talk to me. Let's go for a walk now.

(Both exit)

ACTION: Narrator returns to stage and walks toward set-up # 3. *(Spotlight on set-up #3.)*

NARRATOR: *(Walks over to the clock on the table)* Let's see, what time is it?*[Benjamin Banneker walks in.]* Why, you must be uh - uh Bannaky.

BENJAMIN BANNEKER: Ah - hah. I see you have studied your history. Bannaky was my grandfather's name, who was a member of a royal family in Africa. I am Benjamin Banneker. When I was just 20 years old, I began working on what became the first clock in America.

NARRATOR: So much for C.P. Time. Black folks have always been right on time!

BENJAMIN BANNEKER: Yeah, to make sure things were done on time, I developed an almanac in 1792 that kept track of sunrises, sunsets, tides, eclipses, holidays and it included my own recipes and anecdotes, too.

NARRATOR: An almanac? That seems like a lot of work.

BENJAMIN BANNEKER: Yes it was. Especially since I did all the mathematical calculations myself.

NARRATOR: And what is this? (pointing to a drawing on an easel).

BENJAMIN BANNEKER: Those are the plans and maps of Washington, D.C. I was one of the surveyors to design D.C. and when the Chief Designer left the project and took all the maps and plans, I reproduced them from memory in two days.

NARRATOR: YO! Only two days?! That's incredible!!! Do you have time for hobbies?

BENJAMIN BANNEKER: Why, yes. I spend a lot of time meditating, studying the stars, and reading. He points up in the sky.

(Lights dim.)

> *ACTION*: Narrator looks up, then walks toward set-up # 4. GARRETT MORGAN comes up to the NARRATOR and shakes his hand

GARRETT MORGAN: Hi! I'm Garrett Morgan and I am running for City Council.

> *ACTION*: MORGAN hands a flyer to the NARRATOR who takes it and walks away looking puzzled. He then turns to come back.

NARRATOR: Tell me some more about you!

GARRETT MORGAN: Yes, my platform is:

> 1) Relief for the unemployed and a more efficient administration of public affairs.
> 2) Improved housing conditions.
> 3) Better lighting, police security, and improved sanitation.
> 4) Improved city-owned hospital accomodations.

NARRATOR: And?

GARRETT MORGAN: And I am an active member of the NAACP and publisher of the Call and Post Newspaper printed in Cleveland, Columbus, and Cincinnati, Ohio.

NARRATOR: But aren't you supposed to be an inventor or something in this play?

GARRETT MORGAN: Why yes! I am also an inventor. I invented the Breathing Helmet or Gas Mask used in times of war and by others who have to enter or work in places with dangerous fumes. I have also patented several other inventions.

NARRATOR: Like what?

> *ACTION*: Actors come on stage acting like cars and pedestrians running into each other and around the person on stage with arms to the side (set-up # 4)

GARRETT MORGAN: (pointing to an accident) Once when I was troubled from witnessing a car accident, so I decided to develop electric light signals at intersections to direct traffic.

> *ACTION*: Student holds arms up at shoulder length while cars/persons face them and stop. Then the student imitating traffic light turns one quarter (90°) around with arms down by side and the cars/persons go pass him/her.

NARRATOR: Yo! You invented the traffic light? Well, thank you for letting us <u>stop</u> in on you. Now I've got the <u>green light</u> to <u>go</u> ahead to the next inventor. *(Narrator begins to walk to set-up # 5)*

GARRETT MORGAN: I caution, you should never forget the past for it lights the way to the future.

(Spotlight goes out)

   ACTION: Narrator walks over to set-up # 5.

NARRATOR: Where is the light? What happened to the lights?

LOUIS LATIMER: Perhaps, there is a problem with the carbon filament as the particles transfer to the metallic wires in the incandescent hermetically sealed bulb.

NARRATOR: Say what??! That's okay, don't repeat that. But, you obviously seem to know what you are talking about. Who are you?

LOUIS LATIMER: I am Louis H. Latimer and I designed the carbon filament for the electric light bulb. I am a pioneering inventor in electricity and I have designed manufacturing companies which produce light bulbs as well as street lighting plans for New York City, Montreal, Canada, and London, England. Here, let me show you.

   (LATIMER walks over to the light bulb on the table and clicks it on.) Now you see the light?

NARRATOR: Yes. Would you care to shed light on what else you have done?

LOUIS LATIMER: Certainly. I was the chief draftsman for General Electric and Westinghouse. I drafted the plans for Alexander Graham Bell for the first telephone, I have patented several other inventions myself, and I am a musician and poet.

NARRATOR: Poet? Well, drop some lines on me.

LOUIS LATIMER: With reverence, recognition, and respect for our Ancestors, this poem is called:

Drink to the Dead.

Drink now in silence to the dead.
Those noble souls who've passed away,
Whose promise like the withered flower
Was quenched in premature decay.
Fill up your glasses to the brim;
They would not have our joy the less
Than when they sat among us here
In all their youth and joyousness.
Drink to the souls now passed beyond;
And be our thoughts from sorrow free;
Ring out the praise of those great souls
In one grand earnest symphony;
So that in time, when we are gone
The living may our praise proclaim
And loving lips drink unto us,
To keep alive fond memory's flame.

(Curtain closes.)

NARRATOR: Ase. [ah-shay] (Lights dim.) (Narrator returns to front of stage or wherever he/she was narrating from.)

Scene VI

CHARACTERS

NARRATOR
DR. LLOYD QUARTERMAN
EDITH WILLIAMS
COLONEL FREDERICK GREGORY
DR. PATRICIA COWINGS
DR. GEORGE CARRUTHERS
CHRISTINE DARDEN

NARRATOR: How many of us are familiar with some of these famous personalities? Even fewer of us are familiar with our living legends of African genius in the areas of math, science, and technology. There are many, however, we have chosen to spotlight only a few who are carrying the light today.

DR. LLOYD QUARTERMAN: My name is Dr. Lloyd Quarterman and I am a nuclear scientist. I am one of the six African American scientists and one of the few scientists alive today that was on the team that made the first atomic bomb in 1945. Also, I was in the group that designed the first nuclear reactor made for a submarine. I have done research for over 30 years with radioactive substances. I believe and have stated that "we live in the world of the unknown; that's the only place to live."

EDITH WILLIAMS: My name is Edith Williams and I am a geophysicist. I am one of the first African American women to earn a Masters degree in geophysics. I am thankful for my parents who "taught me to have self-esteem and to work hard, but the most important thing they instilled in me was God."

My training prepares me to help oil companies be more successful at finding deposits. However, I envision myself mining minerals in space, putting them on a shuttle, and sending them back to earth.

COLONEL FREDERICK GREGORY: I am Colonel Frederick Gregory and I am a research test pilot for the U.S. Air Force. I have designed cockpits and invented several improvements to airplanes and the space shuttle including a "single-handed" controller that allows a pilot to control with only one hand. I test piloted the first computer-landing-system planes. I was expected to become the first African American in space, however, I was the first to pilot a space shuttle in space.

DR. PATRICIA COWINGS: I am Dr. Patricia Cowings, a research doctor for the space program. I conduct research on how to keep astronauts well in the weightlessness condition in space. I also develop therapy and exercise programs for each astronaut to deal with the transition from weightlessness to being back on earth. My therapy emphasizes the use of the mind to control sickness.

DR. GEORGE CARRUTHERS: I am Dr. George Carruthers and I am an astrophysicist. When I was in high school, my futuristic ideas were put down by teachers and peers. However, I designed the first camera / telescope used on the moon. My invention, which takes pictures of the Earth's surface and the universe has dramatically changed our knowledge about the planet Earth and the universe.

DR. CHRISTINE DARDEN: I am Dr. Christine Darden and I am an engineer. I am the leading researcher in supersonic and hypersonic aircraft. Hypersonic speed is two or three times the speed of sound - - about two or three thousand miles an hour. I am designing airplanes that will have less sonic boom when they travel. Presently, a supersonic Concorde can fly from London to New York in four hours. I am designing aircraft that will make the trip in just one hour - without a sonic boom.

Scene VII

CHARACTERS
3 FEMALES, 3 MALES

NARRATOR: As our African genius continues to propel us to the stars and beyond, we look forward to a bright future. We, the next generation of African genius, will carry the light and knowledge forward. Let's see what the future will bring.

ACTION: 3 MALES and 3 FEMALES alternately come on stage. Each says:

My name is _____. I am _____ years old and I attend
_____ School. When I graduate, I want to
* _____. (some career or activity related to math, science, and technology.)

Examples:

1) Discover the care for sickle cell anemia.
2) be an astronaut.

ACTION: Other play characters come on the stage.

NARRATOR: You have been a superb audience. We hope you have enjoyed and been enlightened by our play *Math, Science, and Technology: What Africa Has to Say.* From domesticating fire to laser technology; from Imhotep to Dr. Patricia Cowings; from the Moors to Colonel Frederick Gregory, Africa and African Americans have contributed much to the world. We thank you for journeying with us past, present, and future as we have shed some light on:

ALL CHARACTERS: Math, Science, and Technology and What Africa Has to Say!!! ASE!!!

THE END

SUGGESTED READINGS FOR MORE INFORMATION

1) *The Real McCoy* by Frank Forde, Leonah Hall, and Virginia McLean

2) *Black Pioneers of Science and Invention* by Louis Haber

3) *Blacks in Science* Edited by Ivan Van Sertima

4) *They Came Before Columbus* by Ivan Van Sertima

5) *Great Negroes Past and Present* by Russell L. Adams

6) *The African-American Holiday of Kwanzaa* by Maulana Karenga

APPENDIX

Step Pyramid

At least six youth will be needed.

Three (3) get down on their hands and knees in a row.

Two (2) get on the backs of the three actors with their hands and knees.

One (1) actor gets on the top of the two above with one knee and hand on the back of each person.

Backdrop Ideas for Each Scene

I	II	III
corn fields	fruits	plants
river (Nile)	vegetables	step pyramid
fire	baskets	vials
sky & stars	sky & stars	sky & stars

IV	V	VI
Africa	machine	bomb explosion
Caribbean	telescope	oil well
Central America	chemistry lab	space shuttle
boats	almanac	astronauts
sky & stars	pictures of scientists portrayed	telescope/camera
	stop light	sky & stars

- The group can draw or design the backdrop.
- Pay careful attention to the lighting.
- In Scene I, use a cow bell or African bell if you can.

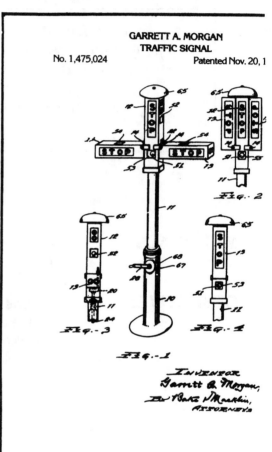

GARRETT A. MORGAN
TRAFFIC SIGNAL
No. 1,475,024   Patented Nov. 20, 1

INVENTOR
Garrett A. Morgan,
By Clark & Mackliu,
ATTORNEYS

One Way To Measure A College

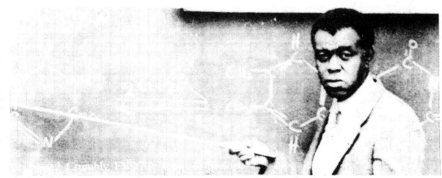

IS BY THE QUALITY OF ITS FACULTY

HARAMBEE TIME # 9

Culture: Beyond the Latest Fads and Fashions

> *"A people without their culture are a people without meaning.*
> *A people without their culture are a people without substance.*
> *A people without their culture are a people*
> *without identity, purpose, and direction.*
> *A people without a culture are a dead people."*
> Haki Madhubuti

MATERIALS: *Lessons From History*
Black Children: Their Roots, Culture, and Learning Styles

OBJECTIVE: To increase your awareness of the elements of African American culture and the fact that this culture grew out of African roots and American experiences. Many of you are only aware of the elements of popular culture that become associated with African Americans such as current fashion trends, slang terminolgy, and popular music.

CULTURE:
Beyond the Latest Fads and Fashions

Culture has been known to provide people with a sense of identity, purpose, and direction.

–9a–HARAMBEE!!! - Work in Harambee groups.

Each group is to list as many elements of African American culture from one of the following categories.

Examples are listed for each category. SETCLAE materials are listed as well as additional secondary sources.

CATEGORIES

1. Family Life (rituals, religion, lifestyle, extended family)

2. Music and Other Art Forms

3. Language, Oral Patterns, and Other Forms of Expression

4. Style (clothing, mannerisms, personality)

5. Holidays, Rituals, and Traditions

EXAMPLES

1. Family Life (rituals, religion, lifestyle, extended family)

Extended family operates so that all children are cared for by grandparents, aunts/uncles, and other family and neighbors.

Children seldom are punished by spankings.

Families get together regularly on certain holidays including Memorial Day, Labor Day, Thanksgiving, Christmas, and Kwanzaa.

Some of the activities are distinctly African American.

2. Music and Other Art Forms

Musicians often improvise by displaying their creativity in a song beyond the written musical notes.

The drum is often central to a performing arts presentation.

3. Language, Oral Patterns, and Other Forms of Expression

Audiences participate and interact with performers. Responses from the audience will include comments, laughter, and phrases such as "Amen!," " Take your time!," "Yeah, you're right!," and "Teach!"

Use of rhyme, rhythm, and body language in communication.

When speaking to an elder, it has traditionally been a sign of respect to avert one's eyes; therefore, eye-to-eye contact is avoided.

4. Style (clothing, mannerisms, personality)

Variety of hairstyles including wearing scarves and turbans, braiding, cornrowing, and dreadlocks.

Ability to respond quickly to change. Includes the use of humor in all kinds of situations.

5. Holidays, Rituals, and Traditions

When African American families get together, the meeting time is always approximate with members arriving as much as one - two hours after the designated time. This concept of time is called C.P.T. (Colored People's Time) and is prevalent in the Caribbean and on the African continent as well.

When African American families get together, the responsibility of preparing food is shared by all. This is an example of the principle UJIMA - collective work and responsibility.

SETCLAE SOURCES (listed for each category)

1. *Lessons,* p. 80, 81
2. *Lessons*, pp. 83, 90-95
3. *Lessons*, pp. 84-85
4. *Lessons*, pp. 86-87
5. *Lessons*, pp. 83, 89

SECONDARY SOURCES

Black Children - Their Roots, Culture, and Learning Styles, Johns Hopkins Univ. Press, 1986, pp. 14-19
Harvesting New Generations, Useni Eugene Perkins, Third World Press, pp. 36-39.
African Religions and Philosophy, John Mbiti, Anchor, NY, 1969

ELEMENTS OF AFRICAN AMERICAN CULTURE

–9b–Record your Harambee circle's list here:

Our Category is _____.

1._____

_____

_____

_____

2._____

_____

_____

_____

3._____

_____

_____

_____

4._____

_____

_____

_____

5._____

_____

_____

_____

6._____

_____

_____

_____

COMMENTS

Which of the elements above are clearly Africanisms?
How has popular culture drawn on elements of African American culture?
How do we maintain, preserve, and practice our various ethnic cultures?
How does culture enhance self-esteem?

RECAPTURE YOUR HERITAGE THROUGH A CULTURAL EXPERIENCE

African Art
African Jewelery
African Fashions

Leather Medallions, Hats Are Stylish Symbols of Black Pride

By Lena Williams
The New York Times

They are throwbacks to the 1960s, recalling the time when the civil rights and black power movements inspired a generation of young black men and women, when everything and anything black was beautiful.

Once again, symbolic jewelry and clothing is being worn by young black Americans making statements of pride and identity: leather necklaces with medallions of red, black and green, some shaped in the outline of Africa, others framing photographs of Malcolm X, Marcus Garvey and Haile Selassie; kufi hats of leather and kente cloth; T-shirts that declare "Black by Popular Demand" or "Black to the Future."

"They're a symbol of us becoming one again," said Andre Lee, an 18-year-old from Washington, D.C., who owns several of the leather necklaces. "It's like the '60s all over again. I like it. I like it a lot. At least it's not that tacky gold stuff."

"It's a whole new style," said Dennis Powell, 20, also of

Washington. "I've seen kids as young as 5 wearing these Afrocentric fashions." Asked what he thought it meant, he said, "It's like that T-shirt. On the front it says, 'It's a black thing.' The back says, 'You wouldn't understand.'"

As with most trends, no one can pinpoint how it started. But two merchants in New York's Harlem, Tyrone Edwards, a native of Antigua, and Lawrence Riley of Trinidad believe it came from the Caribbean.

"A lot of the Caribbean vendors had been making jewelry of leather to sell to tourists," Mr. Edwards said as he stood outside his shop. "When some of the merchants came here, they brought the trade with them."

The leather jewelry sells for $3 to $10, the kufi hats for $15 to $20 and the T-shirts for $5 to $15. Most of the items are sold by private vendors, but with their growing popularity, some smaller department stores now stock them.

While the trend may have started abroad, young black Americans have adopted it most enthusiastically, partly inspired by movies and television.

The wearing of kufi hats was popularized by "Coming to America," in which Eddie Murphy wears several of the West African crown-shaped hats.

And Avery Brooks, the actor in

Eddie Murphy popularized kufi hats in 'Coming to America.' He is pictured with Madge Sinclair, who played his mother in the film.

the television series "A Man Called Hawk," sent youths running to the nearest corner vendor in search of the elaborate African styles he wore on the show.

Rap groups such as Experience Unlimited, Heavy D and the Boys, Kool Mo Dee and Public Enemy — associated with the fad of large gold jewelry — now wear African-inspired jewelry and hats during their performances. So do two of the main characters in Spike Lee's new movie, "Do the Right Thing."

The growing commercialization of these styles disturbs some. "I saw a guy in the mall wearing a T-shirt that had an emblem showing Africa

with bat wings," Mr. Powell said with disgust.

"This is about black heritage," said Joe Eustache, a Trinidadian who sells many of the items from his New York stand. "You've got Korean merchants in Times Square selling this stuff. Stuff they bought from blacks in Brooklyn or Harlem. So it's free enterprise, but there's something there that just rubs me raw."

But others say the message still comes through. "It doesn't matter whether it's a fad or not, if it's something positive," said Darren Grinage, 16.

HARAMBEE TIME # 10

African American Language/Black English:
One of Many Dialects

"We be talkin', but are you listenin'?"
Folami Prescott

OBJECTIVE:
To understand that African American Language, Black English, is a dialect of the English language. It has rules and patterns based on the culture of African Americans and is not bad or inferior to what is known as "standard" English. Both dialects are more appropriate in different settings.

BLACK ENGLISH

Black English is a dialect of the English language. It has rules and patterns based on the culture of African Americans.

All English speaking people speak a dialect of their native language. Other names for dialect are Creole and Pidgin. What other dialects are you familiar with?

–10a–UNIQUE FEATURES OF A DIALECT:

(Examples of Black English in each category are listed)

Pronunciation

    Street is often pronounced "skreet"
    Four is often pronounced "fo"

Word Order

    "Jomo lives in Jamaica" becomes
    "Jomo he live in Jamaica"

    "She's somebody in whom I can believe" becomes
    "She's somebody who I believe in"

Style

    Repetition of a particular statement such as

    "I know you gonna pay me my money back today!"
    "I just know you gonna pay me my money today!"

Non-Verbal Behavior

    The showdown often used inappropriately by African American male students in the classroom.

    Rolling Eyes

Specific Speech Acts

    "Jonin', dissin', soundin', or playin' the dozens" - a non-violent way to express anger or humor. This act of name-calling has become widely acceptable behavior in many circles.

–10b–List situations and settings in which "School/Business English" may be preferred:

1. Job interview   4. _____

2. SAT examination   5. _____

3. _____   6. _____

List situations and settings in which Black English may be preferred

1. With family   4. _____

2. _____   5. _____

3. _____   6. _____

Working in **HARAMBEE CIRCLES**, determine whether each sentence below is written in Black or School English. "Translate" each one into the other dialect. If there are speakers of other

64

dialects in the group, translate some sentences into those dialects with the help of the "expert."

1. He be goin' to school lookin' sharp every day!

2. I have some money in my pocket.

3. He don't look good in that shirt.

4. I have to meet my friends at the library at 4:00.

5. I asked Jabari to come.

6. I like Tameka always come to school with a good attitude.

7. Tanisha is at Stephanie's house.

8. I'mma write somethin' in my journal when I finish my homework.

9. I ast' Rita do she wanna study with us.

MAKE UP YOUR OWN!!!

–10c–Some of the Rules and Patterns of Black English

Note: All speakers of the dialect do not follow all the patterns listed. ADD YOUR OWN!!!

VARIABLE	SCHOOL/BUSINESS ENGLISH	BLACK ENGLISH
Be	She is nice all the time	She be actin' nice all the time
Linking verb	He is going	He goin'
Possessive	John's cousin	John cousin
Marker/Plural Marker	I have five cents	I got five cent(s)
Subject Expression	Jomo lives in Harlem	Jomo he live in Harlem
Verb form	I drank the juice	I drunk the juice
Verb agreement	He reads a lot	He read a lot
Future form	I will help you	I'ma help you
"If" construction	I asked if he did it	I ask did he do it
Negation	I don't have any	I don't got none
Preposition	He is over at his father's house	He over to his father's house
Do	No, he doesn't	No, he don't
Double Consonants	He looks like he's sweating	He look like he sweatin'

Adapted from *The Developmental Psychology of the Black Child* by Amos N. Wilson, Africana Research Publications, NY, 1978, p.148

–10d–"TRANSLATION" EXERCISES FOR THE DIALECT EXPERTS

Each Harambee group is to select one of the selections below and write or speak it in another dialect. Make sure some groups "translate" into School/Business English.

Perform the originals and the translations for family and friends!

Read more Black English in the books listed.

SELECTION ONE

A Negro Love Song

by Paul Laurence Dunbar
{From *Black Voices*, Abraham Chapman, ed., New American Library, NY, 1968}

See my lady home las' night.
                    Jump back, honey, jump back.
Hel' huh han' an' sque'z it tight.
                    Jump back, honey, jump back.
Hyeahd huh sigh a little sigh,
Seen a light gleam f'om huh eye,
An' a smile go flittin' by -
                    Jump back, honey, jump back.
Hyeahd de win' blow thoo de pine,
                    Jump back, honey, jump back.
Mockin'-bird was singin' fine,
                    Jump back, honey, jump back.
An' my heat was beatin' so,
When I reached my lady's do'
Dat I couldn't ba' to go—
                    Jump back, honey, jump back.
Put my ahm aroun; huh wais'.
                    Jump back, honey, jump back.
Raised huh lips an' took a tase,
                    Jump back, honey, jump back.
Love me, honey, love me true?
Love me well ez I love you?
An' she answe'd, " 'Cose I do" —-
                    Jump back, honey, jump back.

SELECTION TWO

Autobiographical Sketch of an Incarcerated Man

{From *Who Took the Weight? - Black Voices From Norfolk Prison*,
Little, Brown & Co., Boston, 1972}

My name is James Shields. I was born in Winston-Salem, North Carolina, November 7, 1945, came to Massachusetts at the age of twelve. I settled in the Roxbury section with my mother, three sisters and three brothers. I attended various schools in Roxbury. I left school to acquire a job to support myself because my mother was unable to get the things I desired, so I became a dropout. But soon I learned that I would need more than ambition and strong desire to work. I was in desperate need of more education in order to live a life of comfort as well as pleasure.

I became interested in writing because I saw a field through which I could present my ideas so that those who may be at the point that I was when I made the wrong decision in my life-style may become conscious through my written thoughts.

I say: We all as people have something to say. Let's open the ears of our minds, because the liberation of our souls comes from the knowledge we intake through the ears of our minds.

SELECTION THREE

Taken from the short story *About Love and Money* in *Some Soul to Keep* by J. California Cooper, St. Martin's Press, 1987.

I got a woman here is a good worker and a good person. Needs a job and will work for a little nothing and live in so she can go to school. I blive she what you need for your problems. I don't blive you'll be sorry. When am I gonna get to visit you?

Love, Me.

Your mother.

SELECTION FOUR

Taken from *The Souls of Black Folk* by W.E.B. DuBois, New American Library, NY, 1969, p. 45

This double-consciousness, this sense of always looking at one's self through the eye of others, of measuring one's soul by the tape of a world that looks on in amused contempt and pity. One ever feels his twoness, an American, a Negro; two souls, two thoughts, two unreconciled strivings, two warring ideals in one dark body, whose dogged strength alone keeps it from being torn asunder.

SELECTION FIVE

Use a selection from a school textbook.

HARAMBEE TIME # 11

Music
The Radio and Rap

> *"When you believe in things
> that you don't understand,
> then you suffer."*
> Stevie Wonder

MATERIALS: tape of popular songs or radio tuned to a popular station
                   Lessons From History

OBJECTIVE: To examine ways that the music we listen to influences our behavior,
                   values, and attitudes.

MUSIC - THE RADIO AND RAP

–11a–WRITING ACTIVITY - Additional paper will be needed.

Take notes on discussion.

Write the name of the song played or your favorite song among the current hits.

Write at least one verse from the lyrics of the song noted above.

List five adjectives that describe how the song made you feel.

1. _____

2. _____

3. _____

4. _____

5. _____

Write a brief essay describing how the music made you feel. Use the five adjectives above in your writing. (Use a separate sheet of paper.)

Try the same exercise with two more songs. (Use additional paper.)

–11b–HARAMBEE!!!

Working in Harambee groups, select one of the following categories. Your group is to discuss the messages in a given song regarding the assigned topic. Report your findings back to the general body.

1 - Love, Sex, and Birth Control
2 - Where to Go to Have Fun
3 - Sharing and Working With Others
4 - The Meaning of Life
5 - Money

Our assigned topic is _____.

The song we chose is _____,

Performed by _____.

–11c–RAP is just one little piece of the African American Cultural Legacy that has its roots in Africa! Listed below are the major areas of African American music. Select one and find out more about it and its artists. A few artists are listed from each category. Listen to it!

1.RAGTIME
Scott Joplin

2. SPIRITUALS & GOSPEL
Fisk Jubilee Singers, The Winans, Andrae Crouch, Tramaine Hawkins

3. BE-BOP
Dizzy Gillespie, Charlie "Bird" Parker

4. BLUES
Muddy Waters, Billie Holiday, B.B. King,

5. JAZZ (African American Classical Music)
Wynton Marsalis, John Coltrane, Betty Carter, Abbey Lincoln, McCoy Tyner

7. JAZZ FUSION
Herbie Hancock, Weather Report, George Benson

8. CONTEMPORARY RAP
M.C. Hammer, Queen Latifah, Public Enemy, Salt 'n Pepa, M.C. Lyte

9. FUNK
Rick James, Parliament, George Duke, Prince

10. HOUSE MUSIC
Steve "Silk" Hurley, Technotronic

11. DISCO
Donna Summer, Chic

12. REGGAE
Bob Marley, Judy Mowatt, Third World, Ziggy Marley

13. RHYTHM & BLUES
Stevie Wonder, Anita Baker, Bobby Brown, Stephanie Mills

FAMILY! Get involved with us with the music!!!

1. Listen to your children's favorites.

2. Become familiar with the artists and the lyrics.

3. Break down the meaning and the styles with your children.

4. Expose your children to other music forms.

5. Create your own lyrics for popular songs with your children.

6. Help your child complete the exercise above.

Use the following chart to record observations made from your favorite music videos. Use a separate sheet for each song.

Song Title_____

Performing artist_____

IMAGES	VALUES PORTRAYED
_____	_____
_____	_____
_____	_____
_____	_____
_____	_____
_____	_____
_____	_____
_____	_____
_____	_____

ADDITIONAL COMMENTS

Why does the media promote music with negative lyrics like "Wild Thing" more than positive lyrics?

How do we get young people interested in music beyond what's played on the # 1 radio station?

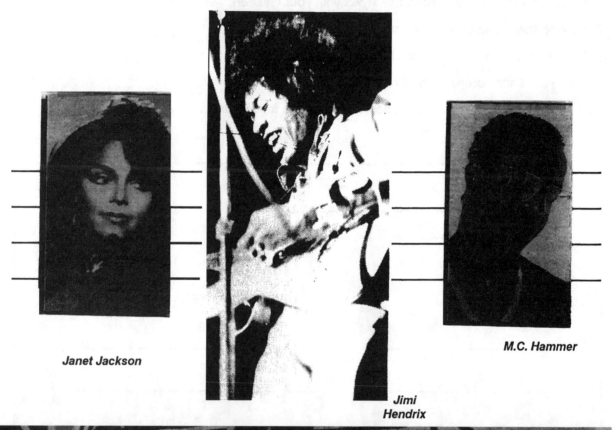

Janet Jackson

Jimi Hendrix

M.C. Hammer

Dizzy Gillespie, Max Roach

–11d–Why would fans want "2 Live Crew" to be "nasty"?

How can we encourage other youth to demand positive and "clean" music by saying "Don't Believe the Hype"?

Can fans influence musicians in terms of the messages they present in their music? How?

2 Live Crew gets away 'clean' after Duluth show

Jonathan Newton/Staff

2 Live Crew's leader, Luther Campbell, a.k.a. Luke Skyywalker, performs before a cheering crowd of 300 Thursday at a Gwinnett teen club.

Group not as nasty as some wanted them to be

HARAMBEE TIME # 12

Public Speaking

> *"Mastery of language affords remarkable power."*
> *Frantz Fanon*

MATERIALS: I.D. card container (Wa On Gozi Kwa Kesho)

OBJECTIVE: To provide you with an audience to practice public speaking skills.

To provide encouragement and constructive criticism to those needing improvement.

PUBLIC SPEAKING

–12a–Why is it important to be an effective public speaker?

Name some settings or situations in which your ability to speak would be important.

    a family reunion
    running for a student government position
    a rap contest (especially without a microphone!)

_____

_____

_____

_____

Criteria for Public Speaking

    Maintain eye contact with audience
    Look around room to address all members of the audience
    Speak loudly (project voice)
    Speak clearly
    Sustain good posture
    Select interesting subject matters
    Keep the presentation interesting and exciting
    Have a sense of humor

_____

_____

_____

_____

Take advantage of the opportunity to speak every chance that you get!!!

–12b–UP FOR DISCUSSION

Who are some of your favorite speakers? Why? Critique them using the criteria listed above.

Rich Mahan/Staff

Charles J. Ogletree moderates a panel on "Ethics and the Human Resource Professional" at the Society for Human Resource Management convention at the Georgia World Congress Center.

Harambee Time # 13

Media: TV, Publications, and Advertising

> *"When you control a man's thinking, you do not have to worry about his actions. You do not have to tell him to stand here or go yonder. He will find his "proper place" and will stay in it. You do not need to send him to the back door. He will go without being told. In fact, if there is no back door, he will cut one for his special benefit."*
>
> Carter G. Woodson

MATERIALS:

Developing Positive Images
Local and national publications
A television and VCR

OBJECTIVE:

To examine the ways that television influences behavior, values, and attitudes.

THE MEDIA: Television, Publications, and Advertising

–13a–WRITING ACTIVITY

Write the names of your three favorites and two least favorites in the area assigned from the five listed below. Then write the reasons why you made these choices. (Use additional paper, or your journals, to expound on your ideas.)

Answer the additional questions as they pertain to your choices.

1. Television Programs
2. Television Commercials
3. Publications (newspapers, magazines, books)
4. Print Ads (found in the publications above)
5. Billboards

MY THREE FAVORITES

1. _____   _____

2. _____   _____

3. _____   _____

MY TWO LEAST FAVORITES (the ones you just don't like at all!)

1. _____   _____

2. _____   _____

How are stereotypes towards women, ethnic groups, age groups, and obesity perpetuated in your selections?

How do your selections influence your behavior?

How do these aspects of media influence your behavior, preferences, and shopping habits?

–13b–TV CRITIC

Name_____ Date _____

Rate every program you watch tonight and five commercials.

Name of Program   **Rating and Additional Comments**

1. _____   _____

2. _____   _____

3. _____   _____

4. _____   _____

5. _____   _____

Use the following letters to rate the programs and commercials.

Write every letter every time that it applies.

    V - VIOLENCE is used as a means of solving problems.
    F - FAMILY is central to the main characters' lives.
    E - Main characters have good EATING HABITS.
    R - Show promotes the importance of treating others with RESPECT.
    L - Shows a LIFESTYLE just like yours (neighborhood, the things you do, etc.)
    S - Behavior, styles, and clothing is SEXUALLY SUGGESTIVE.
    D - DRUGS AND ALCOHOL are being used.

–13c–FOLLOWING THE TRENDS

{FOR MORE INFO: Read *Developing Images*, pp. 52-53, 76-78, *Peer*, pp. 62-63 and the information on pp. 13d-e in this workbook}

Write the brand name of the #1 SELLER in the following categories.

SNEAKER

LINE OF CLOTHING

SODA/SOFT DRINK/POP

MOVIE

Each **HARAMBEE CIRCLE** picks one of these goods and researches the current advertsing approach being taken. Use the chart below.

AMOUNT OF TACTICS USED (sex, signs of wealth, having fun)

ADVERTISING

BILLBOARDS

TELEVISION

PRINT MEDIA

RADIO

PUBLIC RELATIONS (such as sponsoring a concert, youth camp, contest, or poster series)

Blacks Respond Better to Targeted Ads, Study Says

Advertisers Still Unsure On Market Approach

By Jeffry Scott
Staff Writer

A study by a Chicago marketing professor has determined that blacks respond better to television ads aimed directly at them than to ads created for the general market.

That, surprisingly, is something of a shock to Madison Avenue.

At a time when blacks have grown in economic strength — consuming an estimated $200 billion a year in products from soap to malt liquor to automobiles — advertisers still aren't quite sure how to talk to them.

Advertisers' failures can be embarrassing — and expensive.

Entertainers Bill Cosby and Betty Carter combine their musical talents in 'Betty & Bill,' a new television commercial for Coca-Cola Classic.

UP FOR DISCUSSION

How might a decrease in television viewing time affect the buying practices of African Americans as well as others?

RENEE HANNANS/Staff

Black models, like this one on a Colt 45 billboard ad at the corner of Beecher and Cascade roads in Cascade Heights, are being used more often as beer and cigarette companies are switching their advertising campaigns to focus on the black consumer.

Baltimore officials have begun erecting billboards such as this one to promote literacy in an effort to offset the proliferation of 'sin advertising' in black communities.

UP FOR DISCUSSION

What other ways can alcohol and tobacco companies be made accountable to the African American community?

In what ways can the community organize to demand an end to the proliferation of 'sin advertising' in the African American community?

HARAMBEE TIME # 14

UJAMAA:
Cooperative Economics

> *"We must not only be able
> to black [shine] boots, but to make them."*
> Frederick Douglass

MATERIALS: *Motivating and Preparing Black Youth to Work*, pp. 59-65, and 23.

OBJECTIVE: To be able to identify three talents / skills you possess and to develop a business venture based on those skills in your Harambee circle.

HARAMBEE! Work in Harambee groups

–14a–UJAMAA means Cooperative Economics!

Identify three talents you have (use list found on p. 40 in *Motivating Black Youth* for ideas). Then identify a career you would be successful in and a business of your own using these talents.

	Talents	Career	My Own Business

1. _____

2. _____

3. _____

Identify a business your Harambee group would be successful in given everyone's talents and interests. Write down each member's major role / responsibility.

_____

_____

_____

Share completed work sheet with family. Encourage them to support you in following through.

_____

_____

_____

Cooperatives are successful when the Nguzo Saba (Seven Principles) are practiced by its members. The following three are especially important:

UMOJA - Unity

UJIMA - Collective Work and Responsibility

UJAMAA - Cooperative Economics

What kinds of cooperatives would meet your needs?

SITTER SOLUTION

By Maureen Downey
Staff writer

In the economy of babysitting co-operatives, a chit buys more than any check.

"Chits are more valuable than money in Midtown," says co-op member Mary Brown, a mother of twins. "I had a neighbor who bought a secondhand car for 100 chits. I even give them for Christmas gifts."

With grandparents often out of state and teen sitters a scarce commodity, baby boomers are creating co-ops in which friends and neighbors watch each other's children in exchange for chits, or coupons.

"It is wonderful," says Mary White, a management consultant who belongs to a Virginia-Highland co-op whose members mostly have toddlers. "It allows you to have a child over to your house who is the same age as your child. And it is doubly wonderful because you can find a sitter on very short notice."

Co-ops also save money — especially important in view of the $7 hourly rate charged by most professional sitting services.

"You literally never have to spend a cent on babysitting," says Ms. Brown, a seven-year member of the Midtown co-op and vice president of Corporate Child Care Consultants.

Child-care co-ops offer parents a cheap and flexible alternative to babysitters

FOR YOUR INFORMATION

According to the United States Census of Agriculture, in 1923 Black farmers owned approximately 15 million acres of farm land. By 1982, this figure had declined to only 3.2 million acres. Black land owners are currently losing land at the rate of 9,000 acres per week. If this trend continues, there will be no Black-owned land by the year 2000.

The Federation of Southern Cooperatives / Land Assistance Fund (FSC / LAF) has been working in the South for over 20 years to reverse this trend. The FSC/LAF has helped to organize credit unions as well as farmer, home, and craft cooperatives. For more info contact:

FSC/LAF
100 Edgewood Ave. Ste. 228
Atlanta, Ga. 30303
404-524-6882

START YOUR OWN BUSINESS!!!

Based on the ideas developed with your Harambee circle on p.14a, select a service or product that your group will provide as a business. Name the business, develop a business plan, and operate the business.

Here are ideas for each step.

STEP ONE - BUSINESS IDEAS

Serving Our Elders - Some elderly or very busy people need help with grocery shopping, putting out the trash, being escorted through more dangerous parts of the neighborhood, and getting major household chores done like waxing floors, cleaning stoves and attics, or moving furniture.

House Sitters, Inc. - When people go on vacation, they need their mail picked up, plants watered, pets walked and fed, and someone to come by to keep the house from seeming deserted.

Youth Services - Parents need help taking care of their children. Services can include tutoring, babysitting, managing birthday parties, and supervising trips to the pool, skating rink, or even the doctor's office!

Other **SERVICES** you could provide -

> Computer assistance / consulting
> Appliance or Bicycle Repair
> Information Service (finding the information for those who pay a fee as a one-time service or on-going such as free childrens' events)
> Party Planners and Givers
> Office Cleaning
> Planters (decorate and take care of or maintain plants for homes, offices, and other businesses.
> Moving Service
> Interior and Exterior Painting
> Run Errands (of all kinds)
> Secretarial Service

PRODUCTS you could sell -

> Art work. Use themes such as African Art or Art made with natural materials such as wood.
> Tee shirts
> Meals and snack items (especially at festivals and other public events)
> Clothing you make
> Second-hand items

Julian Fuller, President of Best Office Supply

▶ Donna Brooks

President
Brooks, Robinson and Rasheed

STEP TWO - KEY POINTS OF A BUSINESS PLAN

BUSINESS PLAN OUTLINE

Instructions: On separate pages, each Harambee group is to answer in detail each of the following questions. Each response is to begin with the number of the question being answered. Your plan should be complete, grammatically correct (using "Standard English" as a guide), and typewritten.

1. What is the name of your business?

2. Where will you locate your business?

  a Address.
  b. Describe why the building is or is not suitable.
  c. Describe the neighborhood and its advantages and disadvantages for this venture.

3. What are your reasons for picking this location?

4. Is it close to your customers?

What Is Your Product Or Service?

5. Describe your business venture.

  a. What service or products(s) will your business offer?
  b. What will make it special? What will it do that is different from or better than others?
  c. Describe your competitors' strengths and weaknesses.

What Is Your Market?

6. Who are your customers? Describe them.

  a. What are their ages?
  b. What is their income?
  c. How are they changing?
  d. How many potential customers do you have?
  e. Why do your customers need your product or service?

7. How will you attract your customers?

  a. What image do you want your customers to have of your business and how will you develop the image they have of you?
  b. How will you advertise your business?
  c. How will you promote your product / service?

8. What percentage of your sales will be spent on promoting and maintaining sales?

9. How will you set your prices?

What Are Your Finances?

10. What are your start-up costs? (Complete Worksheet No. 1)

11. What is your break even point?

  a. In unit of sales?
  b. In sale of dollars?

12. What are your expenses for the first 12 months?

13. Indicate all sources and amounts of start-up capital. Many small businesses start with money from relatives, friends, or suppliers.

   a. If any amount needs to be repaid, what are the repayment terms?
   b. How much money (capital) do you have now?
   c. What other tangible resources do you have? (Itemize - equipment, materials, tools, etc.)
   d. How much capital do you need?
   e. What will these funds be used for?
   f. When and how will you be able to repay any loans you may secure?

Management

14. If product oriented, how will you buy and control your materials? If service-oriented, how will you organize your work?

15. Develop an organization chart of your company.

16. What are your work plans? Who will perform the tasks? Describe what work functions (work) need to be done and who will be responsible.

17. What controls will you have to:

   a. Identify how actual conditions match or differ from your plan?
   b. Determine what corrective steps need to be taken?

STEP THREE - TIPS ON OPERATING THE BUSINESS OR COOPERATIVE

1. Clearly define each partner's role and responsibilities. Give out job titles if feasible.

2. Set business hours, days, and location(s).

3. Have a meeting for family members to explain the business and how they can support and promote it.

4. Conduct a marketing survey to determine need for the business and current market rates and prices for similar goods and services.

5. Talk to others with similar businesses. Join professional organizations in that area.

6. Be consistent!!!

7. Keep a positive mental attitude (PMA) by encouraging each other, listening to PMA tapes and speakers, and learning about successful business people.

8. Sell something that you believe in!

Charles Blackmon (L), director of the Atlanta Minority Business Development Center (which is funded by the U.S. Dept. of Commerce Business Development Agency) presents an award during MED Week to Helen Willinsky, owner of Helen's Tropical Deluxe

87

WORKSHEET NO. 1

START-UP COSTS

If you are starting a new business or expanding an existing venture, list the following estimated start-up/expansion costs:

Fixtures and equipment $_____
Starting inventory $_____
Office supplies $_____
Decorating/remodeling $_____
Installation of equipment $_____
Deposits for utilities $_____
Legal and professional fees $_____
Licenses and permits $_____
Advertising for the opening $_____
Operating cash $_____
Owner's withdrawal during prep-start-up-time $_____
TOTAL $_____

Type of Equipment	Number Needed	x	Unit Cost	=	Cost
_____	_____		_____		_____
_____	_____		_____		_____
_____	_____		_____		_____
_____	_____		_____		_____
_____	_____		_____		_____
_____	_____		_____		_____

STARTING INVENTORY (Parts And Materials)

Name of Item	Supplier & Address	# Needed	Unit Cost	Other Costs	Total Cost
_____	_____	_____	_____	_____	_____
_____	_____	_____	_____	_____	_____
_____	_____	_____	_____	_____	_____
_____	_____	_____	_____	_____	_____

Identify a business your Harambee group would be successful in, given everyone's talents and interests. Write down each member's major role/responsibility.

Share completed work sheet with family. Encourage them to support you in following through.

HARAMBEE TIME # 15

Who Runs Your Community?

> *"If you are in one boat,*
> *you must learn to row together."*
> South African Proverb

MATERIALS: Community publications

OBJECTIVE: To provide a forum for examining the political, economic, and social
dynamics involved in community organization.

–15a–Who Runs Your Community?

The following is an excerpt from an article entitled *Toward An African American Agenda: An Inward Look* by Ramona Hoage Edelin, Ph.D. Dr. Edelin is the President and Chief Executive Officer of The National Urban Coalition which is an urban action and advocacy organization.

The State of Black America 1990
edited by Janet Dewart
National Urban League, NY, 1990, pp. 181-182.

> *All the research corroborates our experience, that isolation of parts of our groups, such as "drop-outs," "unwed teens," "learning disabled," children, or "senile" senior citizens only increases their inability to function productively in society. The middle class wants a structured way to share talent and advantage with those less fortunate who are of their families and groups, and to reverse the brain drain that depletes our still-segregated cities. Children and young adults often do not have the benefit of an extended family, with seniors or elders who can share wisdom and practical counsel with them. Far too many women ... lack the support network of male and female family and friends who are always needed to help in the raising of children as part of a social or cultural group. Our leadership often goes for extended periods of time without personally relating to the children and families the leaders sincerely seek to represent. And the need for learning and cultural renewal could not be greater. The new model - the 21st Century Model - seeks to prove once again that the whole truly is greater than the sum of its parts, by bonding them all together.*

Listed below are the major components of the model:

1. BUSINESSES - Large and small, offering all of the products and services needed by the group including low- and high-technology, communications and information, manufacturing, entertainment, retail, hospitality, personal grooming, and educational and social-service delivery supports.

2. FAMILY LEARNING CENTER - Early childhood programs, mathematics and science programs, intergenerational activities, strategy club for teens, parenting and home management courses, counseling and health care, entrepreneurship training, and literacy for adults.

3. ADMINISTRATIVE OFFICE BUILDING - Includes conference rooms, training and leadership development institutes, computer center, and satellite communications to other model campuses, schools, businesses, and governmental agencies.

4. RESIDENTIAL DEVELOPMENT - Ranging from one-room apartments to private homes... And we should board the city's foster children and potential dropouts in small clusters with adult leaders.

5. CAFETERIA AND RESTAURANT SERVICES - To support the workers and dwellers of the institutions described above. They must be attractive to the community. Dining rooms - for national and international, private, and political meetings - are included.

6. ATHLETIC FIELDS - Courts, swimming areas, and others. Promotes the personal discipline and team spirit that youth need and fosters fitness, companionship, and relief of stress for adults.

7. ACTIVE CULTURAL CENTER - For presenting talent shows, plays, musical and dance performances, visiting scholars, athletes and entertainers, and children's theater. Artist studios, recording rooms, writers' workshops, radio, television, and newspaper labs, historical societies, and debate clubs should be a part of the cultural center.

Right now, we can and do and must work together where we are and with what we have, to come closer each hour and each day to the future we envision for ourselves.

–15b–HARAMBEE!!! - Work in Harambee groups.

As a group, list the institutions, agencies, and individuals in your community that provide the services in the category assigned to your group. Circle the people that you will interview.

Examples for each category are listed below.

> BUSINESSES - Locally-owned newspaper.

> FAMILY LEARNING CENTER - An independent school (pre-school to 8th grade) that provides evening classes for all ages.

> ADMINISTRATIVE OFFICE BUILDING - A college or university.

> RESIDENTIAL DEVELOPMENT - A private home for teens that are guardians of the state.

> CAFETERIA AND RESTAURANT SERVICES - A community restaurant owned by community members.

> ATHLETIC FIELDS - A city park and recreation center that offers classes taught by community members.

Keysville Mayor Cited for Fight to Revive City Government

Keysville Mayor Emma Gresham gets a congratulatory kiss from state Rep. Tyrone Brooks of Atlanta after she was honored by the Georgia Association of Black Elected Officials on Saturday. Looking on are Cheryl Jackson (left) and Turetha Neely (center).

91

–15c–GETTING TO KNOW MY COMMUNITY

Our Harambee group, _____, has selected the following individual, _____ _____, AND/OR member of the organization _____ to interview.

1. What is your position with the organization?
2. Tell us about the work you do in the community.
3. Have you been involved in the development of other areas described in Dr. Edelin's 21st Century Model? {see article 15a}
4. What are your major concerns regarding community development?
5. In your opinion, who runs this community?

ADD YOUR OWN QUESTIONS

Using the list on p. 15b in your workbook that was devised by your Harambee group, determine which of the seven principles (Nguzo Saba) is exemplified most by the actions of each individual and institution listed. Write them under the appropriate principle. See definitions on p. 80 in *Lessons From History*.

South Atlanta Child Development Center Highlights Academics And Cultural Arts

Ellery Hill

THE NGUZO SABA

UMOJA - Unity

KUJICHAGULIA - Self-Determination

UJIMA - Collective Work and Responsibility

UJAMAA - Cooperative Economics

NIA - Purpose

KUUMBA - Creativity

IMANI - Faith

W.A. Bridges Jr./Staff

Lawrence Shamsid-Deen - Part of the "safety net" for many youth
owner of Supreme Fish Delight restaurants.

JUST FOR FUN

COMPLETE THE ACTIVITY ABOVE USING LEADERS OF YOUR CHOICE!!!

MY SAFETY NET

Draw a safety net and fill it with the appropriate people and organizations in your community. Who would catch you before you fall by the wayside?

> ....*When the home and school fail, children need a community safety net. In most communities safety nets are spearheaded by the business sector. (The business sector not only has the financial resources to respond, but the commitment to its youth and desire to make sure their communities are safe for business growth and expansion is enormous.) In the African American community, when the home and school break down, the lack of the safety net by the church and the business sector has accelerated the number of African American male youth that have become a threat to the people they encounter. I often tell people while my father was my best role model, it was my track coach who created a safety net that prevented me from spending idle time on the streets.*
>
> *We need...a safety net which includes direction, high expectations, employment opportunities, and educational advancement. This may be one of the weakest factors in our communities; our safety net is not strong due to the lack of business development and lack of overall compassion to respond to youth that are not biologically ours, but who belong to the African village. It should be obvious that a single parent and two parents are not going to be as successful as a village raising children.*

> *- Jawanza Kunjufu, Countering the Conspiracy, Vol. III, pp. 56-57*

93

HARAMBEE TIME # 16

Becoming A Real Man/ Woman:
Rites of Passage

> *"When a child learns to wash his hands properly,*
> *he may have dinner with his parents."*
> *Ghanaian Proverb*

MATERIALS:
Countering the Conspiracy to Destroy Black Boys, Vol. III
Herstory
Notebook paper

–16a–MANHOOD / WOMANHOOD

Use the following coding system to note the items that imply manhood or womanhood has been achieved. Write comments next to each item (i.e., the reason why you think the item is important).

MH - sign of manhood
WH - sign of womanhood
MW - sign of manhood and womanhood

_____Having children

_____Washing dishes

_____Crying

_____Hurting someone physically

_____Budgeting one's money

_____Studying regularly

_____Having many friends of the opposite sex

_____Providing for one's children

_____Drinking lots of alcohol and using drugs

_____Having well-developed breasts and hips

_____Owning an expensive car

–16b–RITES-OF-PASSAGE

HARAMBEE! Work in Harambee circles. (Use notebook paper.)

Read *Conspiracy III*, pp. 58-59.

Write the benefits of going through a Rites-of-Passage.

Using the assigned category below, your Harambee circle is to determine the criteria for mastery of that skill or knowledge and suggested activities by which to meet that goal.

You may use *Conspiracy III,* pp. 60-63 and *Herstory*, pp. 119-127 for examples. However, your group must create your own criteria and suggested activities.

The categories are:

AFRICAN AND AFRICAN AMERICAN HISTORY (Substitute appropriate history for other ethnic groups)
ECONOMICS

FAMILY RESPONSIBILITIES
CAREER DEVELOPMENT
SPIRITUALITY
COMMUNITY INVOLVEMENT / LEADERSHIP SKILLS
PHYSICAL DEVELOPMENT / DIET / HYGIENE
NGUZO SABA (A Value System)

Other important categories include:

Self-Reliance (agriculture, construction and home maintenance)
Teen Issues (drugs, sexuality)
Self-Defense

WRITE IT DOWN!!!

Males/females write an essay on what it means to be a man/woman.

African Sisterhood Founded at Spelman College

The African-American men of KMT Fraternity in Atlanta.

96

HARAMBEE TIME # 17

Careers:
More Than Just a J - O - B!

> *"No race can prosper till it learns that*
> *there is as much dignity in tilling a field*
> *as in writing a poem."*
> Booker T. Washington

MATERIALS:

Lessons From History

Motivating and Preparing Black Youth to Work

Magazines (Essence, Ebony, Black Enterprise)

Construction paper

Local newspapers (from the past week)

OBJECTIVE:

To get exposure to many career opportunities and emphasize the potential to succeed in all areas explored.

To prove that drug dealing, sports, entertainment, and the military are not the only viable career options for you to consider.

CAREERS: More Than Just a J - O - B!!!

--17a--HARAMBEE!! (Work in small groups)

STEP ONE

Select five people from the materials listed below. Using the following format, discuss and record the requested information for each person. For more ideas on identifying talents, read *Motivating and Preparing Black Youth to Work*, pp. 39-42.

Lessons From History, Chapters 4 & 5

Magazines - *Ebony, Essence, Black Enterprise,* and *Black Collegian*

Local newspapers

Other biographies in **SETCLAE**

STEP TWO

Select one person (real or fictional) who is pursuing or has begun a career in one of these areas: athletics, entertainment, drugs/crime, or the military. Record the requested information on this person. Use the back of the sheet and other materials to present the information in an eye-catching way. ADD COMMENTS!

An example follows.

NAME	Natalie Cole
Motivation	enjoys entertaining
Career	sings, writes music
Talents	dancing
Training/Education..................	entertainer
Viable Career Options	TV host
Hobbies	singing
Source(s) of Info	ESSENCE OCT. 1990

COMMENT: Natalie Cole underwent six months of treatment for drug abuse in 1983. She solved her problem by "surrounding herself with people who love and support her in ways that are satisfying and fortifying."

–17b–HARAMBEE! Work in your Harambee groups.

Name_____ Date _____

Careers I Can Pursue:

Working in your Harambee group and using any materials available, list as many careers as possible. For each career, list the talents/skills needed to succeed and other steps that must be taken (school/training/experience). Use additional paper if needed.

Careers   What It Takes

1. _____

_____

2. _____

_____

3. _____

_____

4. _____

_____

5. _____

_____

6. _____

_____

7. _____

_____

8. _____

_____

9. _____

_____

10. _____

_____

11. _____

_____

12. _____

_____

On your own!

Select one career that interests you. To find out more, you can:

    a. Read information on the field (in school catalogues, magazines, or books)

    b. Interview someone in the field.

    c. Visit a company that employs people in the field.

    d. Visit a school that trains people in the field.

    e. Ask "experts" in the field.

GET YOUR FAMILY INVOLVED!!!

–17c–FIND YOURSELF A MENTOR!!!

A Mentor is usually an older role model, sponsor, advisor, teacher, or counselor who takes special interest in you.

Mentors can give you inspiration, advice, direction, a shoulder to cry on, and even a job or a loan every once in a while!

In fact, when Folami Prescott wrote her mentor, Dr. Jawanza Kunjufu, to express her admiration and respect for his work and commitment to education and youth, he not only eventually offered her a job, but also offered her an opportunity to co-author SETCLAE with him and work on other ground-breaking projects as well!

HOW TO FIND AND MAINTAIN A RELATIONSHIP WITH YOUR MENTOR

Once you have identified potential candidates for your mentor, write, call, or set up an appointment to meet them and express your interest in spending time with them to learn, meet others in the career field, and be inspired!

Once your mentor states his/her willingness to get involved with your life, make the most of that commitment by doing the following activities on a regular basis!

    1. Discuss your careeer interests and options with your mentor.

    2. Sit in on staff meetings, business meetings, or training sessions with you mentor.

    3. Plan activities with your mentor including museum, restaurant, library, speaking, and other cultural outings.

    4. Have your mentor set up informational interviews for you with his/her co-workers.

    5. Visit professional organizations and community events with your mentor.

    6. Record your most memorable and enlightening experiences with your mentor in a journal.

HARAMBEE TIME # 18

Creative Visualization :
Real Goal-Setting

*"The day on which one starts out
is not the time to start one's preparations."*
African Proverb

WHAT DOES THIS PROVERB MEAN TO YOU?

OBJECTIVE: To be able to see the value of goal-setting. To learn how to set goals and determine all the steps necessary to achieve it. To clarify the difference between short- and long-term goals.

To learn how to visualize your goals.

–18a–GOAL - SETTING

I Want To..So I Will...

*"I have a dream that one day on the red hills of Georgia,
sons of former slaves and the sons of former slave owners
will be able to sit down together at the table of brother-
hood...I have a dream that my four little children will one day live in a nation where they
will not be judged by the color of their skin, but by the content of their character."*

*-Dr. Martin Luther King, Jr.
August 1963, Washington, D.C.*

What might have been King's PLAN OF ACTION towards reaching this grand goal described above?

_____
_____
_____

Write down a short-term goal you have.

_____
_____

Write down your "plan of action" towards reaching that goal.

_____
_____
_____

Write down a long-term goal you have.

_____
_____
_____

What is your PLAN OF ACTION. The plan must include things that you can begin to accomplish immediately.

_____
_____
_____

Use your journal to write down ideas, affirmations, and accomplishments related to reaching your goals.

–18b–CREATIVE VISUALIZATION

Creative visualization is the technique of using your imagination to create what you want in your life. There is nothing new, strange, or unusual about it. You already do it all day every day.

Most of us use our power of creative visualization without even realizing it (in an unconscious way, that is). Unfortunately, we expect problems, difficulties, and other negative happenings in our lives so that is what we often spend time creating for ourselves.

In this session, we will learn how to use our natural creative imagination in a more conscious way to create what we truly want in life whether it involves relationships, school, career, health, beauty, or whatever other goodness your heart desires.

THE KEY TO CREATIVE VISUALIZATION is to use your imagination to create a clear image of something you wish to manifest. Then you keep on focusing on the idea or picture regularly keeping it real in your mind until it actually does become reality.

STEP ONE - SET YOUR GOAL

Decide on something you would like to have, work toward, or create. Examples would be good grades, a job, a change in yourself, improved health, an improved relationship, or a positive attitude toward life. Start with goals that are fairly easy for you to believe in, those that you feel are possible in the near future.

STEP TWO - CREATE A CLEAR IDEA OR PICTURE

Create an idea or mental picture of the object or situation exactly as you want it. Think of it as if it is already existing just the way you want it to be. Include as many details as you can.

STEP THREE - FOCUS ON IT OFTEN

Begin by thinking of the goal in a relaxed, quiet state of mind. Breathing deeply is a very helpful way to get in a relaxed state. Continue to think of your image throughout the day. Focus on it clearly but don't try so hard that you get upset about it.

STEP FOUR - GIVE IT POSITIVE ENERGY

As you create the image of your goal, think about it in a positive way. Make strong positive statements to yourself that it exists, that it has come, or that it is coming to you right now! These statements are called affirmations. When you use affirmations, do not think of any doubts you may have. Practice getting the feeling that whatever you desire is very real and possible.

–18c–POINTS TO REMEMBER

Creative visualization can not be used to bring harm to others. Whatever you try to create for others will always come back to you.

It is very important that you relax when you are first learning to use creative visualization. By being relaxed, you will be able to make many more changes in your life than you will by worrying, planning, and trying to change other people and things instead of concentrating on yourself. Deep breathing is very helpful in reaching a relaxed state.

Group visualization is very powerful. If you are in a group that shares a common goal, visualize reaching that goal by describing it together.

Use affirmations always. Post them in your environment (at home, in school, etc.) Always phrase them in the here and now (I am... I have, etc.) Here are some examples:

...I am studying with my friends and enjoying it.

...I am doing well in school.

...My grades are improving every day.

...I get along well with my friends and associates.

...I am getting along well with my family.

...I have everything I need to enjoy my life.

ACTIVITY IDEAS:

1. Make a treasure map which is a picture of your realized goal. Use photographs, drawings, cards, pictures, and words from magazines, lettering, etc.

2. Visualize your goals presented through speeches, skits, poetry, song, dance, etc.

3. Harambee circles agree on a collective goal and visualize it until it is actualized. They then prepare a report (oral or written) sharing the cause and effect of the visualization process.

4. Create activity ideas in a brainstorming session.

Dan Moore, founder and president of APEX, stands in front of portraits in the museum of late educator. Dr. Benjamin Mays (left) and John Wesley Dobbs, for whom the new building in Phase II of the museum is named.

Sarah Cash
Staff Writer

Dan Moore, the founder and president of the African-American Panoramic Experience (APEX), watches and listens to the school children, smiling to himself.

"That's the best part, watching the children come here," the south DeKalb resident said from his office in the 89-year-old building.

Two Atlanta students recently expressed their thanks after a visit to the black history center on Auburn Avenue.

"I learned a lot on the walk down Sweet Auburn," Tometha Smith said. "Amazing," Yolanda Slaughter said in describing the African art. "I'll cherish the work you have put together all my life."

"You work hard, you labor, you toss and turn at 2 or 3 in the morning," Mr. Moore reflected. "But seeing the reaction of positive things black Americans have done is the most rewarding experience."

As many as 250 school children at a time walk down "Sweet Auburn: Street of Pride," where they can witness almost a century of black history in Atlanta. They see one of Atlanta's first black pharmacies, a barber's chair and other memorabilia from the street termed by Fortune Magazine in 1956 "the richest Negro street in the world."

In an APEX video and tour, they learn of its destruction by fire, its glory days, its decay and more recently its renaissance.

The visitors come not only from Georgia and Alabama, but from Germany, Japan, Australia and West Africa to see what Mr. Moore has assembled for them.

"I decided it would be necessary that Afro-Americans take on the responsbility of interpreting history."

Ten years ago, with only $70, he founded APEX in a tiny Buckhead office. The fledgling museum was moved to an Ashby Street building on loan from Morris Brown College for several years.

In 1985 he moved into the Auburn Avenue two-story building, obtained the loan of an African art collection, which APEX later acquired.

He has helped raise $1.6 million dollars for the museum's first phase, for the restoration and acquisition of its permanent exhibit of African art and for traveling exhibits. He is determined to carve a niche in history.

Mr. Moore is confident that Phase II, raising $20-$25 million and subsequent construction of a 2½-story structure next door will come in two to three years.

APEX's national board plans a 20,000 square foot gallery in the Dobbs building where visitors may walk through replicas of African villages, slave ship and a trading block where slaves were auctioned, among others.

In "The Journey," a 10-000 square gallery, diaramas will revolve visual and audio animatronic figures through a domed chamber, illustrating achievements by discipline such as religion, business, military, law, politcs and civil rights.

WRITING ACTIVITY

List the steps that Dan Moore has probably achieved towards his goal. List the next five steps he must achieve towards reaching his goal to build an African American Panoramic Experience. (APEX)

Use this format for your own goals, too!

ACHIEVEMENTS	OBSTACLES
1. _____	1. _____
_____	_____
_____	_____
2. _____	2. _____
_____	_____
_____	_____
3. _____	3. _____
_____	_____
_____	_____
4. _____	4. _____
_____	_____
_____	_____
5. _____	5. _____
_____	_____
_____	_____

HARAMBEE TIME # 19

Time and How We Spend It

> *I have only just a minute, only sixty seconds in it,*
> *Forced upon me - can't refuse it,*
> *Didn't seek it, didn't choose it*
> *But it's up to me to use it.*
> *Give account if I abuse it.*
> *Just a tiny little minute*
> *But eternity is in it.*
> Benjamin E. Mays

OBJECTIVE: To monitor how time is spent and evaluate how it could be spent more wisely.

–19a–Time and How We Spend It

Record the number of hours you spend doing each of the items listed. The total for each day must equal 24 hours. Add additional categories as needed.

	Mon	Tues	Wed	Thurs	Fri	Sat	Sun	TOTALS
Work	☐	☐	☐	☐	☐	☐	☐	_____
Sleep	☐	☐	☐	☐	☐	☐	☐	_____
School	☐	☐	☐	☐	☐	☐	☐	_____
Television	☐	☐	☐	☐	☐	☐	☐	_____
Sports/Recreation	☐	☐	☐	☐	☐	☐	☐	_____
Music/Partying	☐	☐	☐	☐	☐	☐	☐	_____
Telephone	☐	☐	☐	☐	☐	☐	☐	_____
Chores	☐	☐	☐	☐	☐	☐	☐	_____
Grooming	☐	☐	☐	☐	☐	☐	☐	_____
Family	☐	☐	☐	☐	☐	☐	☐	_____
Study	☐	☐	☐	☐	☐	☐	☐	_____
Daydreaming	☐	☐	☐	☐	☐	☐	☐	_____
TOTAL	___	___	___	___	___	___	___	_____

I didn't realize I spend so much time _____.

I didn't realize I spend so little time _____.

I need to spend more time _____.

I need to spend less time _____.

Name_____ Harambee Group_____

HARAMBEE TIME # 20

DISCIPLINE MEANS SELF-CONTROL!

> *You lit the fire,*
> *now the smoke*
> *hurts your eyes.*
> Tetela (African) Proverb

WHAT DOES THIS PROVERB MEAN TO YOU?

MATERIALS: *Developing Positive Images*

OBJECTIVE: To establish rights and responsibilities and an understanding of the importance of having self-discipline.

–20a–Discipline Means Self-Control!

To provide a format for discussion, we will use the Unity / Criticism / Unity model outlined below. [For more details, read *Developing Images*, pp. 57-59.]

1. Form a Unity Circle.

2. Allow group members to praise each other.

3. Allow group members to offer constructive criticism to each other.

ANYONE WHO HAS AN EMOTIONAL OUTBURST MAY NOT OFFER CRITICISM.*

4. The group member that received the criticism is now asked to share his/her feelings on the issue. At this time, dialogue may occur between the major parties.

5. If action is needed, the group decides what that action will be.

6. End the session with a song or chant.

Today, we will use this format to establish class rights and responsibilities. We will also determine what the consequences will be for those that do not meet the collectively-determined responsibilities.

Additional Activity

The list below is excerpted from a high school Discipline Code. It is a sequence of events that is followed when a student constantly refuses to exercise self-discipline. Discuss the rationale for such actions and suggestions for alternatives that encourage more self-discipline from students.

1. Teacher-student conference

2. Teacher-student-parent conference

3. Teacher-student-parent-administrator conference

4. In-school suspension

5. Class reassignment

6. Suspension

7. Police notification

8. Arrest

9. Expulsion

–20b–OUR RIGHTS AND RESPONSIBILITIES

NAME_____   DATE_____

Put a star next to the three that are most important to you.

RIGHTS	RESPONSIBILITIES
1. _____	1. _____
2. _____	2. _____
3. _____	3. _____
4. _____	4. _____
5. _____	5. _____
6. _____	6. _____
7. _____	7. _____
8. _____	8. _____
9. _____	9. _____
10. _____	10. _____

The above RIGHTS AND RESPONSIBILITIES have been accepted as the BOTTOM LINE EXPECTATIONS WE HAVE FOR EACH OTHER IN THE CLASSROOM.

I agree to respect my own and others' rights by meeting my responsibilities. If I do not, we have decided that the consequences will be:

_____

_____

_____

If you would like to list more Rights and Responsibilties, use the next page.

–20b–(cont.)FOR THE FAMILY

What are the rights and responsibilites for everyone in the household?

RIGHTS

1. _____

2. _____

3. _____

4. _____

5. _____

6. _____

RESPONSIBILITIES

1. _____

2. _____

3. _____

4. _____

5. _____

6. _____

The above RIGHTS AND RESPONSIBILITIES have been accepted as the BOTTOM LINE EXPECTATIONS we have for each other in this family. If someone does not meet them, the consequences will be:

For those that meet them almost always, we will show our appreciation by:

_____

_____

_____

All Family Members sign below and post this sheet in the house.

_____   _____

_____   _____

_____   _____

_____   _____

–20c–MY NEEDS AND WANTS

(There is a difference!!!)

Using the Unity / Criticism / Unity model outlined in section (20a), list your wants and needs. If you PROVIDE IT FOR YOURSELF presently, write an S in the box in front of the item. The S stands for SELF-RELIANCE.

Examples are provided.

NEEDS	WANTS

1. MATERIAL

☐ Food _____   ☐ BMW _____

☐ _____   ☐ _____

☐ _____   ☐ _____

☐ _____   ☐ _____

☐ _____   ☐ _____

☐ _____   ☐ _____

☐ _____   ☐ _____

☐ _____   ☐ _____

☐ _____   ☐ _____

2. EMOTIONAL (Inner Feelings)

☐ Love _____   ☐ Pleasure _____

☐ _____   ☐ _____

☐ _____   ☐ _____

☐ _____   ☐ _____

☐ _____   ☐ _____

☐ _____   ☐ _____

3. CREATIVE (Action)

☐ Male/Female Relationships   ☐ Make Decisions for Myself

☐ _____   ☐ _____

☐ _____   ☐ _____

☐ _____   ☐ _____

☐ _____   ☐ _____

☐ _____   ☐ _____

Teen Mothers Get Second Chance at Success

Seventeen-year-old Dafferneice N. Barge, an honor student who is a sophomore at Carver, visits her 14-month-old napping baby, Quineisha Barge, at the First Step Family Support Project day-care center at the high school.

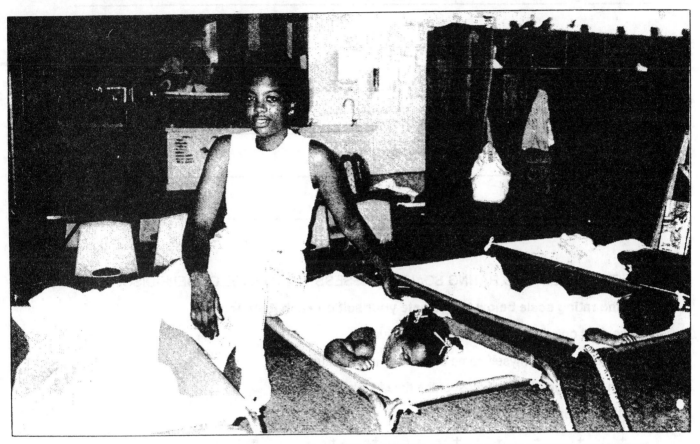

How can developing self-discipline (self-control)
decrease teenage pregnancies and unnecessary acts of violence?

-20d-WHO'S IN CONTROL?
(Checking My Self-Discipline)

List your personal goals (#18) and responsibilities (#20).

"My Personal Goals"

_____1. _____

_____2. _____

_____3. _____

_____4. _____

_____ 5. _____

_____ 6. _____

_____ 7. _____

_____ 8. _____

_____ 9. _____

_____10. _____

USE THE FOLLOWING RATING SCALE TO ASSESS YOUR LEVEL OF SELF-DISCIPLINE!

Use the rating scale below to evaluate your self on each item above.

1. I depend on others for direction in this situation.

2. I am in charge of myself some of the time in this situation.

3. I am in charge of myself most of the time in this situation.

Add the scores for all ten items.

__ + __ + __ + __ + __ + __ + __ + __ + __ + __ =

Write your total score here._____

If your total score is 19 or under, you need to work on improving your ability to exercise self-control.

WRITE IT DOWN!!!

What did you learn about your level of self-discipline from doing the activity above? What are some exercises in self-control you can do to improve your self-discipline? (such as not eating any candy for a week or studying an extra hour a day).

HARAMBEE TIME # 21

Positive People Praising

> *Ashes fly back into the face*
> *of one who throws them.*
> *African Proverb*

WHAT IS YOUR INTERPRETATION OF THE MEANING OF THIS PROVERB?

OBJECTIVE: To be able to find something positive to say about your peers and praise what you like.

POSITIVE PEOPLE PRAISING!!!

–21a–Ways to Spotlight

The following are suggestions on how to spotlight member of your Harambee group (or someone from the general body). Remember the focus is on his/her positive qualities.

Design a bulletin board or poster that spotlights your subject. It can include some or all of the following:

> General biographical information
> Life highlights
> Honors and awards
> Jobs held
> Family life and responsibilities
> Places in which subject has resided
> Future goals (career and otherwise)
> Favorites (book, movie, entertainer, community leader, restaurant, etc.)

Use as many illustrations as possible to make the display colorful, easy-to-read, and interesting.

Put together a TV magazine-style oral report on the student which would include:

- An interview with the featured student
- Interviews with significant others in the student's life.
- Projects in which the student played a part.
- Other interesting related information.

Conduct "group therapy" with the mission being to boost the self-esteem of the selected group member.

Develop a list of ways you could brighten someone's day (gather resources for a research report, have a party at lunch, send a singing telegram, etc.) and let the selected group member choose one. Then have the appropriate group members do it.

A student who exhibits exceptionally positive behavior is "King/Queen For A Day." A strip of kente cloth, a crown, or other African-inspired accessories are worn by the royalty all day.

Sun Spotlight

Attica Lundy

Attica Lundy, a junior at Tri-Cities High School, won the second place trophy and medallion in the Entrepreneurship Written Event.

The state competitive events were conducted in Gwinnett County recently.

Lundy presented a proposal for a tutoring service for kindergarten through third grade to help students who are having trouble with school work.

Lundy is now eligible to compete on the national level in San Jose, Calif., in April.

BE POSITIVE
by Kenneth Zakee

In his book *Revelation to Manifestation*, Self-Published, 1990

I was talking with my papa the other day.
Listen to what he had to say.
You only have one life to live
So why not be positive?

Be positive, think positive, be positive.
Life can be sweet and life can be rough
But these are the things that make you tough.
Be positive, think positive, be positive.
You can't be Sheila E. and you can't be Michael J.
You can't be Madonna and you can't be Prince.
But you can Be positive, Think positive, Be positive.
Believe in yourself and in the Creator.
And then my son you can be the generator
The generator of love, peace, and happiness.

A HA HA
the generator of wealthiness.

Be positive, Think positive, Be positive.
The more you read, the more you know
The more you learn, the more you grow.
Be positive, Be positive, Be positive.
You only have one life to live

So why not be positive?
Be positive, Think positive, Be positive.

Don't bow to defeat but stand up on your feet and
Be positive, Think positive, Be positive.
You are the captain, the captain of your ship.
Get on the ball and get off the stick.
Be positive, Think positive, Be positive.
Words shape people, be careful what you say
Cause if you don't they might come back and
haunt you some day.
Be positive, Think positive, Be positive.
In order to receive you have to give
So why not be positive?

Be positive, Think positive,
Be positive
So Papa said "Son"
I gotta go
but before I do
I just had to let you know to
Be positive, Think positive, Be positive;
Try your very best
and God will do the rest.

HARAMBEE TIME # 22

Defining Friendship

When you know who her friends are,
you know who she is.
African Proverb

OBJECTIVE: To stimulate thought regarding how and why we select friends.

To find ways to handle negative peer pressure.

–22a–DEFINING FRIENDSHIP

How do you choose your friends?

List your criteria for friendship below. In other words, what are the most important things you consider when choosing friends?

Use the categories listed to "get you thinking."

An example is provided for each.

CRITERIA FOR FRIENDSHIP

ACTIONS
(what we do,
how we spend our time.)

Plays basketball.

_____
_____
_____
_____
_____

PERSONALITY TRAITS
(how we act and treat others)

Considerate.

_____
_____
_____
_____
_____

VALUES
(what is important to us)

Likes to buy expensive clothes.

_____
_____
_____
_____

STYLE
(dress, mannerisms,
our walk, our talk)

Curses a lot.

_____
_____
_____
_____

–22b–CHECK IT OUT

Listen to Lemont, a sophomore in a magnet high school in Chicago, IL. Lemont has always been a good student. He wants to be an electrical engineer.

"I can get an A on any test I want. It doesn't matter whether it's biology, algebra, English, history, drafting, or gym. In some of my classes, there have been five tests and I've gotten five different grades, A,B,C,D,F. It's hard being serious the entire year. I've got too many distractions - the fellas, the women, sports, and my music. I could be in honors classes, but I don't want my partners to tease me and call me a fag. I usually sit in the back of the class and clown, and sometimes I don't go to class at all. I'm tight with my friends and the women love me. I don't see the guys respecting the nerds or the women chasing after them. I would like to get A's or B's, it would really get my parents off my back, but I can't be serious for forty straight weeks, plus I'd rather be down with my partners ."

FOR THOUGHT AND DISCUSSION

Do these partners he mentions sound like friends?

What criteria for friendship does Lemont use?

What does Lemont have to do to be down with his partners?

Read more about LEMONT and others in *To Be Popular or Smart* by Dr. Jawanza Kunjufu. Lemont's story is told on pp. 3 - 4.

Many of our youth would rather be popular and cool than smart

In many societies, there is a Council of Elders that people go to for all types of advice. Members of the community know that the elders' experiences make them wise and real smart!

Use your ideas regarding Criteria For Friendship (22a) to respond to one of the following letters to THE ELDERS COUNCIL.

Dear Council of Elders:

> My boyfriend keeps begging me to do the wild thang with him. I keep saying NO because I could get pregnant. He says there are ways around it, but I'm just not interested. Now, he's saying he'll quit me if I don't " give it up". I really love him, but I'm just not ready! What should I do?

Dear Council of Elders:

> All my partners smoke reefer and have tried crack, but I'm determined to stay away from it all. There's a big graduation party coming up and I've told them all I'll get high with them to celebrate going to high school. Should I do it, fake it, or just say no?

Dear Council of Elders:

> Every Monday, me and my best friends "Hook-up" and go hang out in the mall. But my grades are falling and my mom said if she sees one more unexplained absence on my next report card, she's transferring me to another school. How do I handle this?

Dear Council of Elders:

> None of my buddies ever wanna get together and study, but I really want to keep my grades up and I know if they do better in school, it's only gonna help them. How can I convince them we can still hang out and find time to study, too?

Dear Council of Elders:

> One of my partners is becoming a serious "nerd"! He wants to study after school and even on the weekends! When we get on his case, he just says, "Let's just see where I'm at and where you're at in six years!" But, he's still a lot of fun when he's not in the books. Should we just ice him or what?

–22d–

Read the poem aloud. What would be on the author's list of criteria for friendship?

FRIENDS by Abiodun Oyewole

(*Rooted in the Soil* by Abiodun Oyewole, Self-published, NY, 1983)

I am very glad you are my friend
I am very glad I can talk to you
can tell you what I'm going through

When I am walking in the sun
or standing in the rain
drenched in the gray of my feelings

I can't always smile or laugh at myself
I don't always think I'm funny
but joy is in my heart
joy is in my mind
joy is in my name

but I've got to deal with the pain
sometimes I've got to deal with the pain
Because you are my friend
My sky when there is no freedom
My hope when there are no dreams

Because you are my friend
And I trust you with my life
as torn and worn out as it is sometimes
as dusty and rusty as it feels sometimes

there is still enough soul in me
for you to inspire

and for this I will always love you

Friend.

Self-esteem should be the main goal of any relationship.

–22e–WRITE YOUR OWN POEM ABOUT FRIENDSHIP!!!

The following pages include excerpts from the comments of students attending alternative high schools in Atlanta, Ga. Their essays and interview comments appeared in a Drug Abuse Update published by National Families in Action, June 1989, Los Angeles.

GROWING UP WITH DRUGS IN THE STREET

DE'JUAN SHAW

...It is so easy for teenagers to be persuaded to use or sell drugs. You can be pressured to use drugs by a peer. Being pressured by someone that you deal with, associate with, or work with is called peer pressure. Peer pressure is what hits us the hardest as young people. For example, the ways our friends act when they are high might make us want to be high. The things we see our friends with, such as money and fine clothes, might pressure us into wanting to explore that way of life....If I drink, they will accept me; if I don't, they will call me scared, nerd, or give me negative labels...Drug sellers also apply peer pressure....We usually hurt ourselves when we visualize ourselves as someone who wants to make it.

COREY HARPER

...Our actions speak louder than our words. When it comes to the subject of drugs in the streets, we seem to jump at the chance to express our opinions. Teens say that drug use leads to a bad life. They say you shouldn't come in contact with drugs, but they themselves do otherwise. I am a teenager and I fail to understand why so many young people's actions contradict their words...Teens who sell drugs say it's a great way to make fast money when you need it. They don't see there is great risk involved — a chance of being robbed or killed. They don't believe it will happen to them because chance is a normal part of their lives.

Exodus students discuss alcohol and other drug abuse at the National Drug Information Center of Families in Action in Atlanta.

Read more comments on the following page........

125

SUSAN SIMS

...If half the teenagers knew what I have been through in the last few months they would not want anything to do with drugs. I have talked to a lot of my friends and shared my experience with them. They listen and don't mess with drugs because I scared the hell out of them.

TAKEIA THOMAS

I am 16 years old and I am a 10th grader. I have had a lot of experiences with drugs ever since I was age 13. It started when I went to a party with one of my friends. Everybody there was smoking marijuana and drinking alcohol. Instead of saying no when they passed the marijuana around I said yes and ever since that night I have regretted it harshly. I started smoking marijuana and ended up using every kind of drug there is. Once you start, the problems with drugs don't get better, they get worse....

As I look around the world today and see how drugs have taken over young people's lives, it brings tears to my eyes because I can remember once when I was out there the same way. The people I thought were my friends were not. If they were, they would have said no to drugs and would have persuaded me to say no, too.

QUESTIONS FOR DISCUSSION

Why is it so important to be accepted by drug abusing peers?

What other "visualizations" would be more beneficial to us than the ones De'Juan mentions?

Why do we say one thing and do another as Corey states?

Why do we think we will never get hurt?

What do you think Susan told her friends that makes them stay away from drugs?

Why do friends (like Takeia's) push you to use drugs, even if you don't want to, just because they do?

What do you think saved Takeia?

HARAMBEE TIME #23

Relating With My Family

> *"Children are no more separable from their parents than the stripes from the zebra."*
> Angolan Proverb

MATERIALS: *Lessons*, pp. 21-22

OBJECTIVE: To understand and appreciate the value of family in one's life.

To examine the nature of the individual's relationship with family and the living family's connection to its ancestral members.

To examine the effects of slavery on the family.

–23a–
My Search For Roots

Alex Haley (1921 - 1992)

My earliest memory is of Grandma, Cousin Georgia, Aunt Plus, Aunt Liz, and Aunt Till talking on our front porch in Henning, Tennessee. At dusk, these wrinkled, graying old ladies would sit in rocking chairs and talk, about slaves and massas and plantations - pieces and patches of family history, passed down across the generations by word of mouth. "Old-timey stuff," Mama would exclaim. She wanted no part of it.

The furthest-back person Grandma and the others ever mentioned was "the African." They would tell how he was brought here on a ship to a place call Naplis and sold as a slave in Virginia. There, he and a slave woman had a little girl named Kizzy.

When other slaves addressed him as Toby - the name given him by his massa - the African would strenuously reject it, insisting that his name was Kin-tay.

Kin-tay often told Kizzy stories about himself. He said that he had been near his village in Africa, chopping wood to make a drum when he had been set upon by four men, overwhelmed, and kidnapped into slavery.

During 1962, between other assignments, I began following the story's trail. In plantation records, wills, and census records. I documented bits here, shreds there.

Since I lived in New York City, I began going to the United Nations lobby, stopping Africans and asking if they recognized the sounds.

Finally, I sought out a linguistics expert who specialized in African languages. To him I repeated the phrases. The sound " Kin-tay," he said, was a Mandinka tribe surname. And "Kamby Bolongo" was probably the Gambia River in Mandinka dialect. Three days later, I was in Africa.

In Banjul, the capital of Gambia, I met a group of Gambians. In older villages of the back country there are old men, called griots, who are in effect living archives.

Since my forefather had said his name was Kin-tay (properly spelled Kinte), and since the Kinte clan was known in Gambia, they would see what they could do to help me.

I was back in New York when a registered letter came from Gambia. Word had been passed in the back country, and a griot of the Kinte clan had, indeed, been found. I returned to Gambia and organized a safari to locate him.

The old man looked piercingly into my eyes, and he spoke in Mandinka.

"Yes, we have been told by the forefathers that there are many of us from this place who are in exile in that place called America."

Then the man, who was 73 rains of age - the Gambian way of saying 73 years old, based upon the one rainy season per year - began to tell me the lengthy ancestral history of the Kinte clan.

The griot had talked for some hours and had gotten to about 1750 in our calendar. Now he said, through an interpreter, "About the time the king's soldiers came, the eldest of Omoro's four sons, Kunta, went away from his village to chop wood - and he was never seen again..."

Goose pimples came out on me the size of marbles. I got out my notebook, which had in it what Grandma had said about the African.

Later, as we drove out over the back-country road, I heard the staccatto sound of drums. When we approached the next village, people were packed alongside the dusty road, waving, and the din from them welled louder as we came closer. As I stood up in the Land Rover, I finally realized what it was they were all shouting: "Meester Kinte! Meester Kinte!" In their eyes I was the symbol of all the Black people in the United States whose forefathers had been torn out of Africa while theirs remained.

Hands before my face, I began crying - crying as I have never cried in all my life. Right at that time, crying was all I could do.

From "My Search for Roots" by Alex Haley, in Dreamstalkers,
T. Harris et.al., eds. The Economy Co., Oklahoma, 1975.

WRITE IT DOWN!

What thoughts came to your mind as you read this true story?

How would you feel to meet your family members in your homeland?

–23b–My Family Time Line

Make your family time line. Begin by putting yourself on it including birth year and birthplace.

Next, add your siblings. There may be siblings on both sides of you depending on birth dates. Include year of birth and birthplace (city or town and state). You can calculate the birth year as long as you know the family member's age.

Continue in the following order: Parent(s), grandparents, great-grandparents.

Grandparents	Parents	Siblings	Student* (Birth Date)	Present Year	Year 2000

Talk to and write other family members who can help you complete your time line.

Make a list of the family members whom you will contact:
Include addresses and phone numbers.

1. _____

_____

_____

2. _____

_____

_____

3. _____

_____

_____

4. _____

_____

_____

23c
UNITY IN THE FAMILY!!!

Dr. Maulana Karenga, founder of Kwanzaa, gives us the seven levels of unity that offer guidelines for those serious about working towards a united world. One level can not be achieved before the previous one has been achieved on some significant level.

The levels are:

1. SELF

2. FAMILY

3. COMMUNITY

4. NEIGHBORHOOD

5. NATION

6. RACE

7. WORLD

Read the SETCLAE book entitled *Kwanzaa: An African American Holiday* by Maulana Karenga.

Why does the family hold such an important place in the process of striving for unity in the world?

List some examples of unity in the family.

Family rituals build family unity. Family rituals help bring the family together, improve communication, and help members work together in meeting responsibilities. Examples include:

ANNUALLY
Birthdays
Holidays
Death of a loved one
Picnics
Family reunion
School graduations
Vacations

MONTHLY
Library / museum visits
Cultural events
Visits with family members

WEEKLY
Preparation of family meal
Grocery shopping
Attending church
Reading together
Scheduled TV time
Community events
Family meetings

What are some rituals you would like your family to practice?
Ask other family members. Record their answers here.

_____

_____

_____

_____

Plan a ritual that your family could practice in the next week.
Record your plans in your journal or workbook.
Discuss them with your family.

–23d–WHAT'S HAPPENING WITH MY FAMILY?

Take a look at your family. Use the following scale or simply write your own comments on each issue.

    1 - I wish we did.
    2 - We don't and it doesn't matter to me.
    3 - We do some of the time.
    4 - We do most of the time.

___1. Our family does things together on a regular basis.

___2. Our family enjoys doing things together.

___3. There are men that spend time with the family.

___4. We make important decisions together.

___5. I talk to family members about my personal life, (i.e., my relationships and goals).

___6. We take the time to learn about our family tree.

___7. We think the same things are important.

___8. We plan for the future together.

___9. We take the time to praise, help, and support each other.

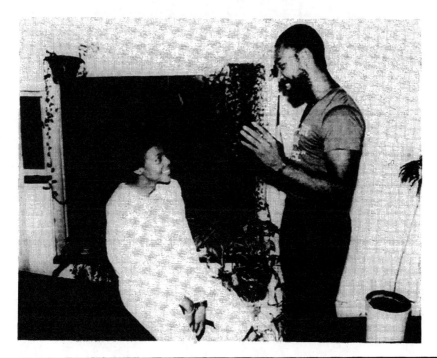

Fathers have special gifts to give their daughters

HARAMBEE TIME # 24

What's Age Got To Do With It?
Respecting Our Elders

> *"It is the duty of the children*
> *to wait on the elders*
> *and not the elders on the children."*
> African Proverb

OBJECTIVE: To appreciate the role of elders in society.

To develop a positive relationship with an elder in your community.

WHAT'S AGE GOT TO DO WITH IT?

–24a–Try This True/False Quiz

1. ____ Most elders can't take care of themselves.
2. ____ There are not many elders in our society as compared to other age groups.
3. ____ Elders get involved in the voting process less than other age groups.
4. ____ Elders hardly ever want to work after reaching retirement age.
5. ____ Most elders are lonely.
6. ____ Many elders hardly attend college or other training programs.

7. Write the number of hours per week of quality time that you spend with an elder. Quality time would include one-on-one conversation, assisting in a household chore or errand, watching television together, or reading together.

TAKE THIS OATH:

I pledge to spend AT LEAST ONE HOUR PER WEEK of quality time with an elder.

All of the items above are FALSE. In other words, they are all MYTHS. Refute these myths by discussing them with elders and those that spend a great deal of time with elders.

–24b–Read the following poem aloud.

THE OLDER I GROW by Abiodun Oyewole
(*Rooted In the Soil*, Self-Published, NY, 1983)

As I grow older
I become more like a child.
my feelings are easier hurt
and although I stand strong
like a rock
only the honey of love
can fulfill my needs.

As I grow older
I become more like a flower
a colorful blossom of sunlight
as soft as a rose
but straight and sturdy
like the stem.

As I grow older
I become more like a sage
turning grains of sand
into mountains
that I climb
to see the reflection
of myself in the river on the other side
and I can feel the breath of Creation

After Church - Grandma and Yakini

135

brushing against my soul
I am more sensitive now

like my skin has been peeled back
and my heart touched with naked fingers

As I grow older
I try to be calm like a stream
and still be fire enough
to create my dream.

UP FOR DISCUSSION

WRITE IT DOWN!!!

What words and thoughts come to your mind when you think of elders?

_____

_____

_____

What will you do with the elder you have chosen to spend at least one hour a week with?

_____

_____

_____

What do you imagine your life will be like as an elder?

_____

_____

_____

–24c–Our Elders - One of Our Greatest Resources

Give concrete examples of elders providing the important resources or information in the areas listed below.

1. Knowledge

_____

_____

2. Wisdom / Advice

_____

_____

3. Living Library

_____

_____

4. Parenting Skills

_____

_____

5. Relationships

_____

_____

As an elder, what kind of people could you help or problems could you solve based on your life experiences?

families

NURTURING OUR ELDERS TELLS THEM WE LOVE THEM

Studies show that older people who can look forward to daily pleasurable experiences tend to lead longer, richer lives. But few of us caught between our work responsibilities and the time we spend with our immediate families, are able to give our elderly relatives the time they deserve. We remember them on birthdays and holidays, but all too often we focus only on their basic survival needs—whether they have a place to live, how well they're feeling, how ofteh they take their medication.

Survival needs are essential, of course, but so are those thoughtful gestures that tell a person she or he is truly loved. Here are some activities you can enjoy with your elderly relatives to show them just how much they are treasured.

Listen to them. We show our elders how much we love them by really listening to what they say, and by respecting their need for independence.

Never patronize elders. Respect their intelligence and integrity as much as you do that of your peers.

Share the past through photographs. Sit down regularly with an older reltive and leaf through her photograph album. Both of you can enjoy her memories and be richer for the experience.

Bring out the "oldies but goodies." No matter how old or young we are, listening to old records can evoke pleasurable memories of our past.

Throw a senior's party. Round up some of your relative's friends and treat them to an afternoon party which hors d'oeuvres, beverages and desserts.

Start a garden. An indoor "garden" on a windowsill or a garden in your front or back yard can provide relaxation and joy for both of you. Leave major decisions to your relative—such as whether fruits, vegetables, herbs, plants or flowers should be grown. If your older relative grew up on a farm, the experience will evoke many rich memories.

Put together a family recipe collection.

Many of us have forgotten (or never learned) how to cook those dishes we loved as children. Invite your relative to your home and ask him or her to give you a lesson.

Give your relative a makeover. Everyone likes to look good, whatever their age. Give your relative a home facial and follow it up with a neck and scalp massage, a shampoo and perhaps a home hair-color job. You may want to finish with light makeup. For a male relative, a home facial and manicure will be appreciated.

Help them display their talents. Many working mothers don't have the time to teach their daughters and sons the fine arts of knitting, quilting and sewing. If your older relative knows one of these skills, encourage her to share them with young family members so that these important arts will not be lost. Or encourage her to form a knitting or quilting club with her friends. If she likes to read or tell stories, set up a weekly story hour so that youngsters can hear an original tale or a chapter from a classic novel.

Excerpts from article in Essence, August 1990

Family gatherings mean good food, good talk and good times. They are also a chance to encourage your children to cultivate new relationships across the age barrier—a perfect complement to friendships they've created within their peer groups.

Sometimes a laugh with folks we love is all we need for our minds and spirits.

Work becomes a pleasure when it gives us the chance to steal a quiet moment together and catch up on family business.

HARAMBEE TIME # 25

Ancestors:
Connecting Us To Our Future

> *The body is earth;*
> *when earthenware breaks*
> *it reverts back to earth.*
> Ethiopian (African) Proverb

WHAT IS YOUR INTERPRETATION OF THE MEANING OF THIS PROVERB?

MATERIALS:

Lessons From History
Shining Legacy
Biographies

OBJECTIVE:

To realize the extremely important value of knowing about your ancestors and using their wisdom and life experiences to guide your life.

–25a–MY ANCESTRAL BOARD OF DIRECTORS

Everyone has ancestors. Ancestors are those that have died. However, once a person dies, their spirit lives on. There are ancestors in your immediate family and ancestors in your ethnic family.

A board of directors is a group of carefully selected people that formulates policy and makes other decisions for the institution they represent. They are often selected based on their expertise in a given area such as financing, computers, or marketing. Boards of directors are not involved in the day-to-day operation of the institution and usually meet monthly, quarterly, or even annually in some cases.

INSTRUCTIONS

Using **SETCLAE** materials and other biographies and historical information, select members of your personal Ancestral Board of Directors. Think of your goals and personality to assist you in choosing ancestors who would provide you with the guidance and models you need to improve your personal life.

At least one ancestor on your board should be a member of your immediate family.

An example is provided below:

Tameka is a shy student with goals of completing high school and going on to college. She became a mother at 16 and never lost her determination to reach her career goals. While raising her daughter, she continues to be a leader among her peers. She is involved in many extracurricular activities including peer counseling.

TAMEKA'S ANCESTRAL BOARD OF DIRECTORS

HER GRANDMOTHER - Died when Tameka was only 12 years old, but Tameka always remembers how hard her grandma worked to keep her family together. She dropped out of high school at the age of 16 to raise her family and Tameka made a pledge she would receive her high school diploma no matter what. After all, she learned about KUJICHAGULIA (self-determination) from her grandmother's example.

MALCOLM X - For moving from a life of crime to a life of outstanding leadership for his people. He moved against the odds just like Tameka.

FANNIE LOU HAMER - For being involved in the Voting Rights Movement. Her grandmother was enslaved. Fannie Lou was a speaker. Tameka will remember her example to overcome her shyness.

–25b–NAMED TO THE BOARD

Can you name the members of this Ancestral Board of Directors and at least one reason why they would be "named to the board"?

Who are the members of your ancestral board of directors and why?

_____

_____

_____

_____

HARAMBEE TIME # 26

The Nguzo Saba:
A Value System

---

*Values are the hinge
on which all human possibilities turn.*
Maulana Karenga

OBJECTIVE: To stimulate thought regarding the behavior, possessions, and desires of the students and the values that relate to them.

HARAMBEE! The Nguzo Saba Seven Values

When your friends want you to play ball or listen to rap music rather than study, what do they value?

When a person sells drugs to children in the neighborhood, what do they value?

When a person helps an elder to the car with his/her groceries, what do they value?

When a female wants a male to spend a lot of money on a date what does she value? When he feels they should have sex because of what he spent, what does he value?

Read the seven values in 26b.

Make sure each Harambee group selects a different value.

Have each group act out a positive and negative demonstration of the Nguzo Saba.

THE NGUZO SABA (Seven Principles)

    UMOJA - Unity

    KUJICHAGULIA - Self-Determination

    UJIMA - Collective Work and Responsibility

    UJAMAA - Cooperative Economics

    NIA - Purpose

    KUUMBA - Creativity

    IMANI - Faith

–26b–FOR THE FAMILY

We are learning about the Nguzo Saba (seven principles). These are seven principles that are a way of life. This "road map for life" is celebrated during Kwanzaa, an African-American holiday celebrated from Dec. 26 - Jan. 1 (see p. 26g for more information). However, the values are quite universal. Live them in all ways that you can.

THE NGUZO SABA - A VALUE SYSTEM

UMOJA - Unity

To strive for and maintain unity in the family, community, nation, and race.

KUJICHAGULIA - Self-Determination

To define ourselves, name ourselves, create for ourselves and speak for ourselves instead of being defined, named, and created for by others.

UJIMA - Collective Work and Responsibility

To build and maintain our community together and to make our sisters' and brothers' problems our problems and solve them together.

UJAMAA - Cooperative Economics

To build and maintain our own stores, shops, and other businesses, and to profit from them together.

NIA - Purpose

To make our collective vocation the building and developing of our community in order to restore our people to their traditional greatness.

KUUMBA - Creativity

To do always as much as we can, in the way we can, in order to leave our community more beautiful and beneficial than we inherited it.

IMANI - Faith

To believe with all our heart in our people, our parents, our teachers, our leaders and the righteousness and victory of our struggle.

Name _____

List seven things you like to do.

	Umo	Uji	Kuj	Uja	Nia	Kuu	Ima
1. _____							
2. _____							
3. _____							
4. _____							
5. _____							
6. _____							
7. _____							

List seven things you personally own.

	Umo	Uji	Kuj	Uja	Nia	Kuu	Ima
1. _____							
2. _____							
3. _____							
4. _____							
5. _____							
6. _____							
7. _____							

Check the box for each principle that is exemplified in your behavior and material posessions.

Discuss your findings in Harambee groups and with the general body.

–26d–JUST FOR FUN!!!

On a blank sheet of paper, write your answers to the following questions.

1. Your favorite place to go

2. Your most valued possession

3. Something you would like to buy

4. A skill or talent you have

5. Your favorite pastime

6. A famous person you admire

Read one of the phrases below filling in the blanks with a classmate's responses. Let students guess whose responses were read.

Phrase I

Yo! What's up? My name is 6_____. I met one of your classmates at 1_____ and s/he had ten 2_____ with him/her. S/he told me that I was his/her idol and it was a dream come true to meet me. S/he said that s/he would do anything to work with me and that I didn't even have to pay him/her any money. Just buy him/her a 3_____. So, I said, Bet! You can be my flunky and you know you'll never have time to 4_____ or 5_____ again! SO what do you think of that?

Phrase II

Answer to this question. If I make a lot of money 4_____ing, should I spend it all on 3_____ or invest it so I'll always have the time to 5_____?

Phrase III

Would you give 6_____ your 2_____ if s/he asked for it?

Phrase IV

Can you think of a way to make money 4_____ing?

Phrase V

Would your family want to 4_____ or go to 1_____ together?

MAKE UP YOUR OWN!!!

Rap or sing the poem below out loud. What is the poem saying about values?

NEW GENERATION

by Abiodun Oyewole

New generation need a new education
about this situation of our lives   (say it 3 times)

Locked in a system
caught in a trap
when you try to get over
you get pushed right back
Don't have no money
to do what you wanna do
and there's a million things
they want to sell to you.

New generation need a new education
about this situation of our lives   (3 times)

and the furs
and the cars
disco lights and the stars
don't mean a thing no no
rockets to the moon
and computerized tunes
don't make you sing no no
For we have found the gold
the mystery is soul
and the rhythm of our love keeps us dancing
through the dark into the dawn.

New generation need a new education
about this situation of our lives   (3 times)

Taken from *Rooted In the Soil* by Abiodun Oyewole,
Self-published, NY, 1983

Write a poem, rap, song, or skit that promotes the Nguzo Saba.

TEEN BUYING POWER

Rich Mahan/Staff

Atlantan Corbin Young, who is 16, tries on a pair of $129 basketball shoes. He says he has 17 pairs of them and buys new ones every two months. Meanwhile, teenage car ownership has jumped since just last year.

Adolescents today have billions to spend

IN THE MONEY: A survey shows teens spent $55.9 billion last year on day-to-day needs, vs. $25.3 billion in '75.

By Mariann Caprino
The Associated Press

NEW YORK — Comedian Jay Leno tells a joke about how a parent punished her teenager by sending him to his room.

Big mistake. The kid should have been sent to the parent's room, a place devoid of the accouterments of youth, like CD boom boxes or high-tech sneakers.

Mr. Leno delivers the punch line in a TV commercial for Doritos, but as an increasing number of businesses are discovering, today's teens are in a position to buy far more than tortilla chips. Controlling more cash than the thirtysomething set can imagine, many adolescents are downright affluent, and they're playing a part in big-ticket purchases like never before.

"They're not buying just fast food, soft drinks and dime-store makeup anymore," said Peter Zollo, who heads Teenage Research Unlimited in suburban Chicago. They are "significantly more confident in their ability to buy big-ticket items than they were just one year ago," he said.

Indeed, teen car ownership is up nearly 13 percent for new vehicles and 9 percent for used vehicles, compared with 1989 levels, according to Mr. Zollo's survey of more than 2,000 people between the ages of 12 and 19.

Nearly half of all teens own their own television sets, compared with just 29 percent a decade ago, and about 20 percent own videocassette recorders, the New York market research firm Rand Youth Poll found.

- What do our spending habits say about our values?

- How can we use this buying power to live and promote the Nguzo Saba?

148

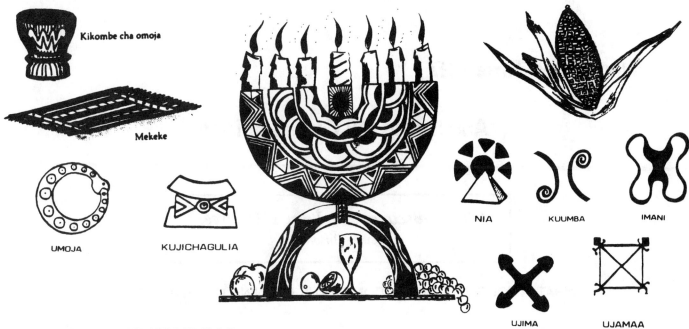

Kikombe cha omoja

Mekeke

UMOJA

KUJICHAGULIA

NIA

KUUMBA

IMANI

UJIMA

UJAMAA

–26g–ACTIVITY IDEAS

1. Working in Harambee groups, think of at least one example of how the group lives each principle in school, home, or other settings. Record your results.

2. Write a Kwanzaa play.

FOR THE FAMILY

HARAMBEE!! (Let's Pull Together!)
PAMOJA TUTASHINDA!! (Together We Will Win!)

HOW TO CELEBRATE KWANZAA (Dec. 26-Jan. 1)

1. Decorate your home with pictures of leaders, the liberation flag (red, black, and green) African art, and the seven items listed below:

    MKEKA - straw mat - symbolizes the foundation of African tradition and history.

    KINARA - candle holder - symbolizes the parent stalk.

    MISHUMAA - seven candles - symbolizes the seven principles.

    MUHINDI - ears of corn - represents children, our most valued treasure.

    ZAWADI - gifts - symbolizes rewards for correct actions. They should be hand-made, books, or purchased from an African American business.

    MAZAO - fruit and other "crops" - represents the fruits of our labor.

    KIKOMBE - unity cup - symbolizes our oneness of purpose.

2. Discuss the principle of the day with your family at dinner or some other time.

3. Attend community events such as plays, storytelling, and lectures.

4. Have a POT LUCK affair with family and friends on KUUMBA.

5. Spend IMANI with the family reflecting on the past year and planning the year ahead.

    During Kwanzaa, greet everyone with the words HABARI GANI?! (What's the news?) The response is the principle of the day.

Harambee Time # 27

Assessing My Qualifications

> *When I discover who I am, I'll be free.*
> *Ralph Ellison*

WHAT IS YOUR INTERPRETATION OF THE MEANING OF THIS QUOTE?

MATERIALS: Index cards
Small container or envelope
Biographies
Lessons From History
To Be Popular or Smart

OBJECTIVE: To begin the bonding and "getting to know me" process by assessing your skills and documenting your personal background.

To understand and accept the uniqueness of self.

ASSESSING MY QUALIFICATIONS
(Who Am I?)

–27a–Use *Lessons From History*, pp. 53-65 and *To Be Popular or Smart*, pp. 1-9 for ideas to complete the following exercise.

Ideas for an Autobiographical Sketch

An autobiographical sketch can include:

1. Your early childhood: Where you were born, how your family came to live there, what family members lived with you at that time, your earliest memories, your favorite games, toys, and pastimes.

2. Significant school experiences: Memories from day care/kindergarten, a time in school when you were angry, excited, proud, disappointed, motivated, etc.; what you always remember about elementary and middle/jr. high school, and your favorite teachers.

3. Summers: Places you visited, water experiences, new friends made, old friends you got to know better, how you spent most of your time, family members you spent time with and what you did when there was nothing to do.

4. Superlatives: Your favorite book, movie, famous person, family member, places to go, your best friend, what you like most or least about life, career(s) that interest you the most, etc.

5. Culture and History: Most significant experiences, knowledge, or influences related to your ethnic history and culture i.e., leaders, movements, literature, music, media, dance, art, communication, foods, beauty, family, etc.

Duafe (the wooden comb). *One of the very few representational forms in adinkere patterns.*

Kontire ne Akwam (elders of the state). *"Tikorommpam" (One head does not constitute a council.)*

"Nkyin kyin (ohema nkyinkyin)". Changing one's self; playing many roles.

Adinkra symbols (found on pgs 70-71 in Shining Legacy) represent various aspects of the lifestyle and culture of the African peoples of West Africa. They are used in making fabric, artwork, and carvings and have a special meaning.

6. The Future (what type of contribution would you like to make to your race?) Where you would like to live, how you see marriage and parenthood in your future, your relationships with family members, how far you plan to go in school, careers you may consider exploring, other things you'd like to do, the kind of lifestyle you'd like to lead, what kind of friends you'll have, how your lifestyle will differ from or be similar to that of your present friends.

7. Other important Experiences: Illnesses, travel, special gifts, holiday experiences, birthdays, death of a loved one, joining an organization, appearing before an audience, graduations, family changes (divorce, marriage, babies, people moving in and out of your household), awards and achievements, moving, changing schools, meeting someone special, getting in serious trouble.

The autobiographical sketch can be presented as:

An oral presentation
Pictures
An interview format
A speech
A dialogue
A short story, song, or poem

THERE ARE NO LIMITS TO YOUR CREATIVITY!

Ideal for a Historical Artifact

Create an artifact that, if found 100 years from now, would describe your personality, accomplishments, and other traits. Examples include:

A speech you wrote
A picture you drew
A self-portrait
A newspaper article about some event in which you were involved
A letter to or from you
An oral story that can be passed down through family and friends
A song or poem you wrote or like a great deal

What would an author write about you in a biographical sketch?

Walter Massey (1939 -)

Walter Massey enjoyed math and science as a child. A graduate of Morehouse College, he once said, "I began to see that physics was a way to use mathematics to try to understand the world and that was very exciting." Massey is the first African American to be president of the American Association for the Advancement of Science, the world's largest science organization. He has been a professor in physics and director of Argonne Laboratory. His research lies in measuring the energy of certain liquids and solids. Walter is also the President of Morehouse College.

Protesters Claim Morris Brown Students Expelled

BARRY WILLIAMS/Special

Flanked by Tony Smith (left), a Georgia State student, Derrick Boazman (right) leads a march Monday night to the Morris Brown College president's home. Mr. Boazman was among eight students arrested May 1 during a campus protest.

By Pat Burson
Staff Writer

About 30 people — many of them students from Morris Brown College and other schools in the Atlanta University Center — protested outside the home of the Morris Brown president, Dr. Calvert Smith, Monday night because they say several students who were arrested during a demonstration in May have been expelled.

Derrick Boazman, a 23-year-old former student government president at Morris Brown, led a brief march from the front of the school on Martin Luther King Jr. Drive to the president's home at 601 University Place N.W. He was joined by Morris Brown alumni Michael Langford, project coordinator for the United Youth Adult Conference (UYAC) and Tony Muhammad, a member of the Nation of Islam.

Nearly a dozen young men — dressed in khaki jumpsuits, red berets and army boots, referred to as "soldiers" by Mr. Muhammad — marched at each side of the group as it moved toward the Mr. Smith's house, singing "This Little Light of Mine."

"I for one have been expelled," Mr. Boazman said. "The [other] students have been throughout this summer phased out. At this point we haven't had an audience with the board or the administration. This is a grave injustice, and we won't stand by, ... as they make closed-door decisions that affect all our lives."

In April, Morris Brown students held a demonstration after college officials threatened to expel about 150 students who were behind on tuition payments.

Mr. Boazman was among 27 people — including eight Morris Brown students — charged with criminal trespass in a May 1 protest when they refused to leave the college's student center follow-ing the administration's decision to cancel a concert by rap group Public Enemy.

Following the incidents, the administration agreed to demands to improve campus security, improve the quality of the food and upgrade sanitary conditions, and introduce more black studies into the curriculum. They also agreed to form student committees to investigate the quality of health care on the campus, dormitory conditions and planned increases in tuition charges.

One school official who watched the Monday night protest from a safe distance said he did not understand the student's complaints.

"Their concern's have been addressed. We have a new security force, the food is better, the dormitories have been painted," said Tyrone Fletcher, dean of admissions.

HARAMBEE TIME # 28

SCHOOL: Education For What?

> *"Knowledge is better than riches."*
> *African Proverb*

MATERIALS: *Lessons From History*
                   To Be Popular or Smart
                   Developing Positive Images
                   Miseducation of the Negro

OBJECTIVE: To explore the benefits of school, your perceptions of its value, and how it could be better in your opinion.

                   To recognize education as a primary means of achieving life's goals.

SCHOOL: EDUCATION FOR WHAT?

–28a–WRITING ACTIVITY

Why do some students think it's cool to be popular but not cool to be smart or do well in school?

_____

_____

Vincent Fitzgerald's game "Zorbow" is one way to make school more relevant and learning more fun!

Makes Math Fun Numbers Game

By Sonia Murray
Staff Writer

Teachers have tried for years to trick kids into learning basic math. Apples and oranges just haven't done the trick.

The Atlanta public schools think Zorbow may.

When classes start Monday, 30,000 first- through sixth-graders will enter the age of Zorbow — a galactic adventure with numbers that was invented by More-house College senior Vincent Fitzgerald.

Zorbow is the name of a fast-paced match card game designed to let kids test their math skills, regardless of ability. The object is predictable enough: to match correct solution cards to math problems. What makes it different is that, at opportune times, players shout strange, otherworldly names such as "Cycon," "Nuclo" and — at game's end — "Zorbow!"

Morehouse senior Vincent Fitzgerald with Zorbow, the mathematics game he invented.

RICH MAHAN/Staff

155

MAKING SCHOOL MORE RELEVANT

HARAMBEE! Work in Harambee circles.

Develop some concrete suggestions for making school more relevant and interesting. Offer them to teachers, principals, consultants, like the SETCLAE authors of African American Images, and others.

Each group may use the following core information and other available resources:

Group # 1 - *Peer,* Chapter 1

Group # 2 - *Peer,* Chapter 2

Group # 3 - *Conspiracy II*, Chap. 4 with emphasis on p. 33

Group # 4 - *Developing Images*, Chapter 3

Group # 5 - *Peer,* Chapter 5

OUR RECOMMENDATIONS

Share your recommendations with the principal, school board members, parents, and other concerned parties.

Send them to:

African American Images
1909 W. 95th Street
Chicago, Illinois 60643

WE WANT TO HEAR FROM YOU!!!

–28b–Following is the format for the five sessions that will be for Parents and Peers. Create your own flyers and handouts for the sessions.

SESSION I

For Parents Only

Parents have a dialogue to begin to answer the question "Why do some youth think it's cool to be popular but not cool to be smart?" Some of the reasons are:

1. Racism
2. Effects of slavery
3. Inferior schools
4. Lack of African history
5. Negative definitions of Blackness
6. Job availability (or lack thereof)

Have the parents address the following questions:

1) How do you act White?
2) How do you act Black?
3) Where are your roots?
4) Describe the achievements in ancient Egypt.
5) What is the difference between Negro and African history?
6) What is good hair and pretty eyes?
7) Explain how one-third of African Americans earn over $25,000 and another one-third earn less than $5,000.
8) Which career offers the best chance for income, stability, and growth: sports, crime, education, music, drugs, or owning your own business?

SESSION II

For Parents and Peers

Watch the video *To Be Popular or Smart* if possible. Then begin the discussion of where youth attribute their success and failure. In this session, ask your teenager the following questions.

1) Are you better in sports or academics?
2) Why do you do well in this area?
3) What do you do when you don't do well?
4) When you don't do well in this area, how do you explain your failure?
5) What will you do about it in the future?

SESSION III

For Parents and Peers

In this session, ask the youth to explain why Asian Americans outscore African Americans on tests. Some of the factors are:

a) Racism

b) Mental slavery

c) Inferior schools

d) Test bias

e) Lack of exposure to history and culture

f) Poor parental support

g) Inadequate study time

Make sure the discussion includes television viewing habits and the following information:

	Avg. SAT Scores	Avg. Study Time
Asian Americans	939	12 hrs.
European Americans	933	8 hrs.
African Americans	757	5 hrs.

SESSION IV

For Parents and Peers

In this session, the discussion should be around exploration of career possibilities. Youth are to name at least one occupation for each letter of the alphabet. Try to create a game out of it. Bring in guest speakers to describe their professions.

SESSION V

For Parents and Peers

1) List the designer in order of your preference regarding gym shoes, pants, shirts, blouses, and dresses.

2) If you had a million dollars and had to spend it to benefit African American people, how would it be disbursed?

3) Design a monthly budget based on the needs of a single adult and a realistic salary.

Peers

DEVELOP YOUR OWN IDEAS TO CONTINUE THE DISCUSSIONS AND THE PARENTAL INVOLVEMENT AND SUPPORT IN YOUR EDUCATION!!!!!!!!

UP FOR DISCUSSION

Write it down!!!

How can extended family meet the needs of African American male students that other family members are not able to meet?

What role does culture play in this "weeding out" process? ("Weeding out" refers to the phenomena that results in African American males being placed in Special Education, detention, or suspension in greater numbers than any other group.)

How can you help turn this situation around for the better?

Read *Countering the Conspiracy to Destroy Black Boys, Vol. II*, Chapters 2, 3, and 4 to understand this phenomena.

TEN CRITICAL QUESTIONS
(WHAT EVERY STUDENT WILL KNOW AFTER SETCLAE)

1. Who am I?

2. Where did my people originate?

3. When did the history of my people begin?

4. What have my people contributed?

5. What is the culture of my people?

6. Who oppressed my people?

7. How was it done? (oppression of an African people)

8. How did my people respond?

9. What is the present condition of my people?

10. What can I do to enhance the condition of my people?

The SETCLAE Student Profile

High School/Post-Secondary

Instructions

Please answer the following questions on the answer sheet and think real hard about how you really feel before answering each one. THERE ARE NO RIGHT OR WRONG ANSWERS. We want YOUR answers.

Part I

Read each statement or question. If it is true for you, select the answer "a" on the answer sheet. If it is not true for you, select the answer "b". Answer every question even if it's hard to decide. (Just think about yourself and what's important to you.) Select only one answer for each question.

1. I like to be alone sometimes.	a. Yes	b. No
2. I enjoy public speaking.	a. Yes	b. No
3. Cleaning up should be done collectively.	a. Yes	b. No
4. School will help me to accomplish my own goals.	a. Yes	b. No
5. I enjoy looking for positive things to say about people.	a. Yes	b. No
6. I have personal goals.	a. Yes	b. No
7. I would rather do an extra credit project by myself than with a small group.	a. Yes	b. No
8. I get upset when things don't go my way.	a. Yes	b. No
9. School is boring most of the time.	a. Yes	b. No
10. I speak more than one dialect.	a. Yes	b. No
11. If I don't see a trash can, I throw my trash on the ground.	a. Yes	b. No
12. I like participating in special projects like science fairs and quiz bowls.	a. Yes	b. No
13. When the truth is hard to say, I don't say it.	a. Yes	b. No
14. My friends are more important to me than my family.	a. Yes	b. No
15. My neighborhood is a good place to live.	a. Yes	b. No
16. I can get any job I want if I work at it hard enough.	a. Yes	b. No
17. I like being with people that are different from me.	a. Yes	b. No
18. I like me!	a. Yes	b. No
19. I believe I can have my own business when I get older.	a. Yes	b. No

161

20. The contribution I make to the world is not as important as the contributions of some other more famous people.   a. Yes   b. No

21. African Americans have not made many achievements in math, science, technology, and business.   a. Yes   b. No

22. If I could, I would make friends with people of all races.   a. Yes   b. No

23. Black people are not able to compete with others in many areas.   a. Yes   b. No

24. I want to be able to speak standard English in certain situations.   a. Yes   b. No

Part II

Read each item carefully. If it is something that is important to you, select the "a" on the answer sheet. If it is not important to you (it doesn't really matter or has nothing to do with you), select the "b" box. Take your time and think about it. There are no right or wrong answers. We want to know your feelings.

1. Helping others

     a. Important to me   b. Not important to me

2. What others think of me

     a. Important to me   b. Not important to me

3. Reading in a study group

     a. Important to me   b. Not important to me

4. Television as a way to receive most of my information

     a. Important to me   b. Not important to me

5. Solving problems by fighting

     a. Important to me   b. Not important to me

6. Learning about my family Members - dead and living

     a. Important to me   b. Not important to me

7. Working with others on short- and long-term projects

     a. Important to me   b. Not important to me

8. Doing whatever my friends do

     a. Important to me   b. Not important to me

9. Wearing expensive clothes

     a. Important to me   b. Not important to me

10. Doing well in school

     a. Important to me   b. Not important to me

11. Speaking up for myself and my ideas

        a. Important to me   b. Not important to me

12. Being positive most of the time

        a. Important to me   b. Not important to me

13. Living conditions in Africa

        a. Important to me   b. Not important to me

Part III

Read each statement carefully. Read the choices. Then select "a" if the statement accurately describes you and your feelings. Select "b" if the statement does not accurately describe you and your feelings.

If asked to describe my personality to someone I'd never met, I would use words like:

1. a community organizer   a. Yes   b. No

2. confident   a. Yes   b. No

3. mature   a. Yes   b. No

4. critical of others   a. Yes   b. No

5. proud of my culture   a. Yes   b. No

6. easily bored   a. Yes   b. No

Africa is a dark continent filled with hunger, poverty, and ignorance.

        a. True   b. False

I can list five living African American men that are doing positive things in their families, businesses, churches, communities, or some other organization.

        a. Yes   b. No

List them below.

1. _____

2. _____

3. _____

4. _____

5. _____

Select the one that is most important to you. Choose only one!

        a. Being popular   b. Doing well in school

Part IV

Read the following statements and choices for answers carefully. Then pick the answer that most accurately describes your feelings.

There are NO RIGHT OR WRONG ANSWERS. Choose the answer that is right for YOU.

1. When my friends have fun without me, I
    a. am happy they are having fun.
    b. don't even think about it.
    c. wish they weren't having fun without me.

2. When I hear something negative about a person, I
    a. can't wait to tell someone else.
    b. talk to the person to see how I can help.
    c. try to find out more, because it's interesting.

3. When someone says something about me that is not good but is true, I
    a. get upset.
    b. don't want to be around them anymore.
    c. listen and learn from their observations.

4. When someone makes fun of me, I
    a. get upset.
    b. am hurt.
    c. laugh with them.
    d. make a joke of it.
    e. don't like it.

5. When I am talking to someone, most of the time I look
    a. at their hands.
    b. into their eyes.
    c. at the floor.
    d. all around.

6. I make sure I am neat and clean in my appearance.
    a. never
    b. once in a while
    c. most of the time
    d. always

7. Money is important for:
    a. buying expensive clothes.
    b. building the community we live in.
    c. buying whatever I want.
    d. saving for future plans.

8. A girl becomes a woman when (select the answer that is most important to you.)
    a. she has a baby.
    b. her body becomes more developed (she has breasts.)
    c. she takes care of herself and her family.
    d. she can talk back to her mother.
    e. she has a boyfriend.

9. When I do poorly on my schoolwork, I
   a. don't really care.
   b. know I tried my best.
   c. know I should try harder.
   d. know it's only because I can't do any better.
   e. know the teacher gave us work that was too hard or boring.

10. In my involvement with organizations, I
   a. like to hold a leadership position.
   b. like to work as a team.
   c. don't like doing the dirty work.
   d. often disagree with other members.

11. When I need help, I
   a. get frustrated.
   b. ask for it.
   c. try to figure it out myself.

12. I pick my friends because
   a. they look good.
   b. they are cool.
   c. they are understanding.
   d. they have something to offer me.

13. I am glad I am the race I am.
   a. Yes
   b. No

14. I chose the answer above because
   a. I am proud of my heritage.
   b. I should be glad.
   c. I study my history and culture.
   d. my friends say it's important.

15. I like my favorite music because
   a. of its rhythm for dancing.
   b. of its positive messages.
   c. of its ability to help me relax.
   d. the rappers curse and dog out the women.
   e. the videos are nice.

16. A boy becomes a man when
   a. he can handle drugs and crime.
   b. he makes a baby.
   c. he takes responsibility for his actions.
   d. he can fight well.

17. When I attend assemblies or special events, I like to sit
   a. in the middle of the auditorium.
   b. in the front of the auditorium.
   c. in the back of the auditorium.

18. When I set a goal, I
    a. expect someone to make it happen for me.
    b. plan how I will do it and make the first step.
    c. just think about it real hard.
    d. ask my friends to get me started.

19. When the teacher leaves the room, I
    a. talk.
    b. stop doing my work.
    c. look at who is being disobedient.
    d. find something quiet to do once I finish my work.

20. I like my favorite television program because
    a. it's real funny.
    b. I enjoy the action.
    c. I enjoy the "scenery" (cars, clothes, houses, etc.).
    d. it is educational.
    e. it makes me think and discuss important issues with others.

21. Learning about one's culture and heritage is very important and helps me feel good about who I am.
    a. Yes
    b. No

22. Check the attributes that make you think of beauty.
    a. light skin
    b. dark skin
    c. natural hair
    d. long hair
    e. thin shape

23. Answering these questions was
    a. very enjoyable.
    b. no big deal.
    c. a good way to take a closer look at my personal development.
    d. a waste of time.

24. Africa has many cities.

                    a. True   b. False

25. Africa is the Motherland of Black people all over the world.

                    a. True   b. False

26. Egypt, also known as Kemet (which means Land of the Blacks), is in Africa which is the cradle of civilization.

                    a. True   b. False

27. African people have always resisted domination all over the world.

                    a. True   b. False

28. Africa is mostly jungle.

                    a. True   b. False

29. Tarzan movies show you what Africa is like and used to be like.

                a. True   b. False

30. Africa is a continent on which there is a cultural unity more important than the differences we hear about in the news.

                a. True   b. False

Using the definitions on the right, place the corresponding letter in the space provided that you feel best fits each of the seven principles listed (Nguzo Saba).

__ 31. UMOJA

a. to build our stores and businesses to profit from them together.

__ 32. KUJICHAGULIA

b. to have a collective goal of building and developing our community.

__ 33. UJIMA

c. being creative in the way we make our communities better all the time.

__ 34. UJAMAA

d. being determined to speak up for myself.

__ 35. NIA

e. to work on challenges collectively and feel responsible as a group.

__ 36. KUUMBA

f. to believe in ourselves and that we will do great things.

__ 37. IMANI

g. to keep in touch with and offer support to friends, neighbors, and community.

Photo / Reference Credits

(Number refers to the Harambee Session)

1. Chicago Defender, June 16, 1990,
   Fast Forward,
   Herstory: Black Female Rites of Passage

2. To Be Popular or Smart
   Atlanta Journal Constitution, June 8, 1989

3. Cleveland Plain Dealer, May 21, 1989
   Talking Drum, March/April 1990

4. Lessons From History
   Atlanta Journal, January 31, 1989

5. Fast Forward, July 1989
   Color Me Light of the World
   Lessons From History

6. Lessons From History

7. Atlanta Journal, 1990

9. Atlanta Journal, August 1, 1989

11. Atlanta Journal, March 2, 1989
                 June 15, 1990

12. Atlanta Journal, 1990

13. Atlanta Journal, March 26, 1989

14. Atlanta Journal, September 25, 1990
    Fast Forward, Oct. 1989
                 April 1990

15. Atlanta Journal, January 29, 1989
                    August 22, 1989
    Atlanta Constitution, June 15, 1990

16. Countering the Conspiracy to Destroy Black Boys, Vol. II
    Fast Forward, July 1990
    Talking Drum, March 1990

18. Atlanta Journal, June 8, 1989

19. Herstory
    Motivating Black Youth to Work

20. Atlanta Journal, June 8, 1989

21. Southside, April 26, 1989

22. To Be Popular or Smart
    Herstory
    Drug Abuse Update, June 1989

23. Choosing A Path
    Herstory

24. Essence, August 1990

25. Yusuf Rasheed, Artist, Health News, Faiz Institute, Feb. 1990

26. Atlanta Journal, June 28, 1990

27. Lessons From History
    Atlanta Journal & Constitution

28. To Be Popular or Smart
    Atlanta Journal & Constitution

SETCLAE PRONUNCIATION GLOSSARY

KISHWAHILI

ASANTE SANA	(ah - SAN - tay - sah - na)	Thank you very much
BENDERA	(Ben - DER - ah)	Flag
HABARI GANI	(ha - BAR - ree - GAH - nee)	What's the news?
HARAMBEE	(ha - ROM - bay)	Let's pull together
HOFU NI KWENU	(HO - foo ni KWAY - nu)	My concern is for you
HUJAMBO	(hu - JAHM - bow)	Hello
IMANI	(ee - MAH - nee)	Faith
KARAMU	(kah - RAH - moo)	Feast
KIKOMBE CHA UMOJA	(ki - KOM - bay cha oo - MO - jah)	Unity cup
KINARA	(Kee - NAH - rah)	Straw mat
KUJICHAGULIA	(KOO - jee - cha - goo - LEE - ah)	Self-determination
KUUMBA	(Koo - OOM - bah)	Creativity
KWANZAA	(QUAN - zah)	African-American holiday (Dec. 26-Jan. 1)
MAZAO	(mah - ZAY - oh)	Crops
MISHUMAA SABA	(mee - SHOO - mah SAH - bah)	Seven candles
MKEKA	(m - KAY - kah)	Straw mat
MUHINDI	(mu - HEEN dee)	Dried corn
MWALIMU	(Mwa - LEE - mu)	Teacher
MWANAFUNZI	(Mwa - na - FUN - zee)	Student
MZURI	(m - ZU - ree)	Good
NIA	(Nee - ah)	Purpose
NGUZO SABA	(n - GOO - zo - SAH - bah)	Seven principles
NJEMA	(n - JAY - ma)	Fine
PAMOJA TUTASHINDA	(Pa - MO - jah TOO - ta - shin - dah)	Together
SIJAMBO	(SI - JAHM - bow)	Response to hujambo (hello)
UJAMAA	(oo - JAH - mah - ah)	Cooperative economics
UJIMA	(oo - JEE - mah)	Collective work and responsibility
UMOJA	(oo - MO - jah)	Unity
WA ON GOZI KWA KESHO	(wa uhn GO - zee kwa KAY - show)	Tomorrow's leaders
ZAWADI	(zah - WAH - dee)	Gifts

WORDS FROM OTHER AFRICAN LANGUAGES

ASHANTI	(ah - SHAHN - tee)	community in West Africa
CHAGGA	(CHAH - gah)	community in East Africa
DOGON	(DOE - gohn)	community in West Africa
JENNE	(jen NAY)	city in West Africa
OLUDUMARE	(OH - loo - doo - MAR - ay)	Supreme Being
YORUBA	(YUR - uh - buh)	community in West Africa
ZULU	(ZOO - loo)	community in South Africa